LIVING LANGUAGE®

SPANISH
COURSEBOOK

REVISED & UPDATED

THE LIVING LANGUAGE® SERIES

Living Language Basic Complete Courses, Revised & Updated

Spanish*
French*
German*
Portuguese (Brazilian)
Portuguese (Continental)
Inglés/English for Spanish Speakers

Japanese*
Russian
Italian*

Living Language Intermediate Skill Builder Courses

Spanish Verbs
German Verbs

French Verbs
Italian Verbs

Living Language Advanced Courses, Revised & Updated

Advanced Spanish   *Advanced French*

Living Language Ultimate™
(formerly All the Way™)

Spanish*
French
German
Italian
Russian
Japanese
Inglés/English for Spanish Speakers
Advanced Inglés/English for Spanish Speakers
Chinese
Portugese

Advanced Spanish
Advanced French
Advanced German
Advanced Italian
Advanced Russian
Advanced Japanese

Living Language® Essential Language Guides

Essential Spanish for Healthcare
Essential Spanish for Social Services
Essential Spanish for Law Enforcement
Essential Language Guide for Hotel & Restaurant Employees

Living Language® English for New Americans

Everyday Life
Health & Safety
Work & School

Living Language Fast & Easy™

Spanish	Italian	Portuguese
French	Russian	Czech
German	Polish	Hungarian
Japanese	Korean	Mandarin
Arabic	Hebrew	(Chinese)

Inglés/English for Spanish Speakers

Living Language All Audio™

Spanish* French* Italian* German*

Living Language American English Pronunciation Program

Fodor's Languages for Travelers

Spanish   French   Italian   German

Living Language® Parent/Child Activity Kits

Learn French Together
Learn Italian Together
Learn Spanish Together
Learn French Together: for the Car
Learn Italian Together: for the Car
Learn Spanish Together: for the Car

Living Language English for the Real World

for Chinese Speakers
for Japanese Speakers
for Korean Speakers
for Spanish Speakers
for Russian Speakers

*Available on Cassette and Compact Disc

If you're traveling, we recommend
Fodor's guides

Available in bookstores everywhere, or call 1-800-726-0600
for additional information.

Visit our website at www.livinglanguage.com

SPANISH
COURSEBOOK

REVISED & UPDATED

REVISED BY IRWIN STEIN, PH.D.

Director of Language Programs

Department of Spanish and Portuguese

Columbia University

◆

Based on the original by

Ralph Weiman and O. A. Succar

LIVING LANGUAGE®
A Random House Company

This work was previously published under the titles *Conversation Manual Spanish*, *Living Language™ Conversational Spanish*, and *Living Language™ Conversational Spanish, Revised and Updated* by Ralph Weiman and O. A. Succar.

Published by Living Language, A Random House Company, New York, New York.

Living Language is a member of the Random House Information Group

Random House, Inc New York, Toronto, London, Sydney, Auckland

www.livinglanguage.com

Living Language and colophon are registered trademarks of Random House, Inc.

Printed in the United States of America

Library of Congress Catalog Card Number: 55-12164

ISBN 0-609-80288-7

10   9

CONTENTS

INTRODUCTION	xv
INSTRUCTIONS	xvi

LESSON 1 — 1
A. The Letters and Sounds — 1
B. Some Vowel and Consonant Sounds — 3

LESSON 2 — 4
A. Cognates: Words Similar in English
   and Spanish — 4
B. Special Sounds — 4

LESSON 3 — 7
A. The Spanish Alphabet — 7
B. Regional Differences in Pronunciation — 7

LESSON 4 — 9
A. Vowels — 9
B. Diphthongs (Common Vowel Pairs) — 11

LESSON 5   12
  A. Consonants   12
  B. More English-Spanish Cognates   17
  C. General Spelling Equivalents   19

LESSON 6   21
  A. Days and Months   21
  B. Numbers 1–10   22
  C. Colors   22
  D. Seasons and Directions   23
  E. Morning, Noon and Night; Today,
     Yesterday, Tomorrow   23
     QUIZ 1   23
  F. Word Study   24

LESSON 7   25
  A. Greetings   25
  B. How's the Weather?   27
     QUIZ 2   28

LESSON 8   28
  A. Where Is . . . ?   28
  B. Can You Tell Me . . . ?   29
     QUIZ 3   30
  C. Do You Have . . . ?   30
  D. In a Restaurant   31
     QUIZ 4   33

LESSON 9   34
  A. To Speak: *Hablar*   34
  B. The and A   37
     QUIZ 5   38
  C. Contractions   39
  D. Plurals   39
  E. Adjectives   40
  F. Possessive "de"   40
  G. Asking a Question   41

H. Not   41
REVIEW QUIZ 1   41

LESSON 10   43
A. May I Introduce . . . ?   43
B. How Are Things?   45
C. Good-bye   46
QUIZ 6   47

LESSON 11   47
A. To Be or Not to Be: *Ser, Estar*   47
QUIZ 7   50
B. It Is   50
QUIZ 8   51
C. To Have and Have Not: *Tener*   52
D. Word Study   53

LESSON 12   53
A. I Only Know a Little Spanish   53
B. Do You Speak Spanish?   55
QUIZ 9   57
C. Excuse Me and Thank You   58
D. Word Study   59

LESSON 13   60
A. This and That (Demonstrative
Pronouns and Adjectives)   60
QUIZ 10   61
B. More or Less   61
C. And, Or, But   62
D. Word Study   63
QUIZ 11   63
REVIEW QUIZ 2   64

LESSON 14   66
A. Where?   66

B. Here and There   66
C. To the Right, etc.   69
D. Near and Far   69
    QUIZ 12   70

LESSON 15   71
A. I, You, He, etc.
   (Subject Pronouns)   71
B. It's Me (I), You, He, etc.   72
C. It and Them
   (Direct Object Pronouns)   72

LESSON 16   73
A. My, Your, His, etc.
   (Possessive Adjectives)   73
B. Its, Mine, Yours, His, etc.
   (Possessive Pronouns)   77
C. Prepositional Pronouns   79
D. Direct and Indirect Object Pronouns   80
E. Myself, Yourself, Himself, etc.
   (Reflexive Pronouns)   84
F. Word Study   86
    QUIZ 13   86
    REVIEW QUIZ 3   87

LESSON 17   89
A. Some Action Phrases   89
    QUIZ 14   90
B. Can You Tell Me?   91
C. Word Study   91

LESSON 18   92
A. Numbers   92
B. More Numbers   94
    QUIZ 15   95
C. Word Study   96

LESSON 19 96
    A. How Much? 96
    B. It Costs . . . 96
    C. My Address Is . . . 97
    D. My Telephone Number Is . . . 98
    E. The Number Is . . . 98

LESSON 20 98
    A. What's Today? 98
    B. Some Dates 99
    C. To Go: *Ir* 100
    D. Word Study 101
    QUIZ 16 102

LESSON 21 103
    A. What Time Is It? 103
    B. At What Time? 104
    C. It's Time 105
    D. Time Expressions 105
    QUIZ 17 106

LESSON 22 106
    A. Yesterday, Today, Tomorrow, etc. 106
    B. Morning, Noon, Night, etc. 107
    C. This Week, Next Month,
       In a Little While, etc. 107
       QUIZ 18 110
       REVIEW QUIZ 4 111
    D. Word Study 113

LESSON 23 114
    A. No, Nothing, Never, Nobody 114
    B. Neither, Nor 116
    C. Word Study 117

LESSON 24 117
    A. Isn't it? Aren't they? etc. 117

B. Some, Any, a Few   119
   QUIZ 19   120
C. Like, As, How   121
   QUIZ 20   122

LESSON 25   123
  A. Have You Two Met?   123
  B. Hello, How Are You?   124

LESSON 26   126
  A. Glad to Have Met You   126
  B. So Long   128
   QUIZ 21   129
  C. Visiting Someone   129
   QUIZ 22   131
  D. Word Study   132

LESSON 27   133
  A. Please   133
  B. Excuse Me, I'm Sorry   134
   QUIZ 23   135
  C. Some Useful Verbal Expressions 136
   REVIEW QUIZ 5   137
  D. Word Study   139

LESSON 28   140
  A. Who? What? When? etc.   140
   QUIZ 24   143
  B. What a Surprise! What a Pity!
   How Awful! How Nice!   144
   REVIEW QUIZ 6   144
  C. Word Study   147

LESSON 29   148
  A. It's Good   148
  B. It's Not Good   148

QUIZ 25   150
C. I Like It   150
D. I Don't Like It   151
E. I Had a Good Time!   152
QUIZ 26   152

LESSON 30   153
A. In, To, From, etc.   153
B. Word Study   158
QUIZ 27   158
QUIZ 28   159
QUIZ 29   160

LESSON 31   162
A. On the Road   162
B. Walking Around   163
C. Bus, Train, Subway, Taxi   165
QUIZ 30   168

LESSON 32   169
A. Writing and Mailing Letters   169
B. Faxes and Telegrams   170
C. Telephoning   170

LESSON 33   173
A. What's Your Name?   173
B. Where Are You From?   174
C. How Old Are You?   174
D. Professions   176
E. Family Matters   178
F. Word Study   179

LESSON 34   179
A. Shopping   179
QUIZ 31   184
B. General Shopping Expressions   185

LESSON 35   185
  A. Breakfast in a Restaurant   185
     QUIZ 32   189
  B. To Eat: *Comer*   191
  C. A Sample Menu   192

LESSON 36   192
  A. Apartment Hunting   192
     QUIZ 33   198
  B. To Have: *Tener*   199
     QUIZ 34   202
  C. To Have (Auxiliary): *Haber*   202
  D. To Do, to Make: *Hacer*   204
     QUIZ 35   206

LESSON 37   206
  A. Could You Give Me Some Information?   206
     QUIZ 36   212
  B. Sight-Seeing   214

LESSON 38   215
  A. The Media and Communications   215
  B. At the Airport   216
     QUIZ 37   218
  C. The Most Common Verbs
  and Their Forms   220

LESSON 39   228
  A. What's in a Name?   228
  B. Notes on Names in Spanish   231

LESSON 40   232
  A. Fun in Spanish   232
  B. Important Signs   237
     QUIZ 38   239
     FINAL QUIZ   239

SUMMARY OF SPANISH GRAMMAR — 243

1. The Alphabet — 243
2. Pronunciation — 244
3. Stress — 245
4. Punctuation — 246
5. Some Orthographic Signs — 247
6. The Definite Article — 248
7. The Indefinite Article — 250
8. Contractions — 251
9. The Days of the Week — 251
10. The Months of the Year — 252
11. The Seasons — 253
12. Masculine and Feminine Gender — 253
13. The Plural — 256
14. The Possessive — 256
15. Adjectives — 256
16. Position of Adjectives — 259
17. Comparison — 261
18. Pronouns — 263
19. Position of Pronouns — 267
20. Conjunctions — 269
21. Question Words — 270
22. Adverbs — 271
23. Diminutives and Augmentatives — 275
24. Demonstratives — 276
25. Indefinite Adjectives and Pronouns — 278
26. Negation — 279
27. Word Order — 279
28. Tenses of the Verb — 280
29. Conditional — 285
30. Subjunctive — 287
31. Commands and Requests
    (the Imperative) — 293
32. The Participle — 298
33. Progressive Tenses — 300
34. Passive Voice — 301
35. To Be — 301

THE FORMS OF THE REGULAR VERBS   305
  A. Conjugations I, II, III   305
  B. Radical Changing Verbs   308
  C. Regular Verbs with Spelling Changes   312

THE FORMS OF THE IRREGULAR VERBS   324

LETTER WRITING   334
  A. Formal Invitations and Responses   334
  B. Thank-You Notes   336
  C. Business Letters   337
  D. Informal Letters   339
  E. Forms of Salutations and
    Complimentary Closings   340
  F. Form of the Envelope   345

INTRODUCTION

Living Language® Spanish makes it easy to learn how to speak, read, and write Spanish. This course is a thoroughly revised and updated version of *Living Spanish: The Complete Living Language Course®*. The same highly effective method of language instruction is still used, but the content has been updated to reflect modern usage and the format has been clarified. In this course, the basic elements of the language have been carefully selected and condensed into forty short lessons. If you can study about thirty minutes a day, you can master this course and learn to speak Spanish in a few weeks.

You'll learn Spanish the way you learned English, starting with simple words and progressing to complex phrases. Just listen and repeat after the native instructors on the recordings. To help you immerse yourself in the language, you'll hear only Spanish spoken. Hear it, say it, absorb it through use and repetition.

This *Living Language® Spanish Coursebook* provides English translations and brief explanations for each lesson. The first five lessons cover pronunciation, laying the foundation for learning the vocabulary, phrases, and grammar, which are explained in the later chapters. If you already know a little Spanish, you can use the book as a phrase book and reference. In addition to the forty lessons, there is a summary of Spanish Grammar, plus verb charts and a section on writing letters.

Also included in the course package is the *Living Language® Spanish Dictionary*. It contains more than 20,000 entries, with many of the definitions illustrated by phrases and idiomatic expressions. More than 1000 of the most essential words are capitalized to make them easy to find. You can increase your vocabulary and range of expression just by browsing through the dictionary.

Practice your Spanish as much as possible. Even if you can't manage a trip abroad, watching Spanish movies, reading Spanish magazines, eating at Spanish restaurants, and talking with Spanish-speaking friends are enjoyable ways to help you reinforce what you have learned with *Living Language® Spanish*. Now, let's begin. The instructions on the next page will tell you what to do. *¡Buena suerte!* Good luck!

COURSE MATERIAL

1. Two 90-minute cassettes or three 60-minute compact discs.

2. *Living Language® Spanish Coursebook.* This book is designed for use with the recorded lessons, but it may also be used alone as a reference. It contains the following sections:

   Basic Spanish in 40 Lessons
   Summary of Spanish Grammar
   Verb Charts
   Letter Writing

3. *Living Language® Spanish Dictionary.* The Spanish/English–English/Spanish dictionary contains more than 20,000 entries. Phrases and idiomatic expressions illustrate many of the definitions. More than 1000 of the most essential words are capitalized.

INSTRUCTIONS

1. Look at page 1. The words in **boldface** type are the ones you will hear on the recording.

2. Now read Lesson 1 all the way through. Note the points to listen for when you play the recording. The first word you will hear is **Alicia.**

3. Start the recording, listen carefully, and say the words aloud in the pauses provided. Go through the lesson once and don't worry if you can't pronounce everything correctly the first time around. Try it again and keep repeating the lesson until you are comfortable with it. The more often you listen and repeat, the longer you will remember the material.

4. Now go on to the next lesson. If you take a break between lessons, it's always good to review the previous lesson before starting a new one.

5. In the manual, there are two kinds of quizzes. With matching quizzes, you must select the English translation of the Spanish sentence. The other type requires you to fill in the blanks with the correct Spanish word chosen from the three given directly below the sentence. If you make any mistakes, reread the section.

6. Even after you have finished the 40 lessons and achieved a perfect score on the Final Quiz, keep practicing your Spanish by listening to the recordings and speaking with Spanish-speaking friends. For further study, try *Living Language®️ Spanish 3, Living Language®️ Ultimate Spanish* and *Ultimate Spanish Advanced,* as well as *Living Language®️ All Audio Spanish.*

LIVING LANGUAGE®

SPANISH

COURSEBOOK

REVISED & UPDATED

LESSON 1

A. THE LETTERS AND SOUNDS

1. Some Spanish sounds are like English. Listen to and repeat the following Spanish names and notice which sounds are similar and which are different:

Alicia[1]	Alice	**Luis**	Louis
Alfredo	Alfred	**Luisa**	Louise
Antonio	Anthony	**Manuel**	Emanuel
Carlos	Charles	**Miguel**	Michael
Carmen	Carmen	**María**	Mary
Enrique	Henry	**Pedro**	Peter
Elisa	Elizabeth	**Pablo**	Paul
Francisco	Francis	**Pepe**	Joe
Fernando	Ferdinand	**Pilar**	Pilar
Isabel	Elizabeth	**Rafael**	Ralph
Juan	John	**Ramón**	Raymond
Juana	Jane[2]	**Rosa**	Rose
Juanita	Jennie	**Ricardo**	Richard
Jorge	George	**Roberto**	Robert
Julio	Jules	**Vicente**	Vincent
Julia	Julia	**Violeta**	Violet
José	Joseph	**Virginia**	Virginia

NOTE:

 a. that each vowel is pronounced clearly and distinctly.
 b. that a single consonant is pronounced with the following vowel.
 c. that consonant blends (fr, dr, bl, gl, etc.) are pronounced with the following vowel.

[1] Words in boldface are on the tape.
[2] Or Joan.

d. that the accent mark (´) shows the syllable that is stressed. Sometimes, however, it serves merely to distinguish words:

él he   *el* the
sí yes   *si* if

2. Now listen to some place names:

Barcelona	Nevada
Buenos Aires	Río Grande
Colorado	Río de Janeiro
Gibraltar	Santa Fe
La Habana	San Fernando
Las Vegas	Sierra Nevada
Los Angeles	Tampico
Madrid	Veracruz
Montana	

3. Now a few country names:

Argentina	Honduras
Brasil	Inglaterra
Colombia	México
Cuba	Nicaragua
Chile	Puerto Rico
Costa Rica	Panamá
Estados Unidos	Perú
España	Portugal
Francia	El Salvador
Guatemala	Venezuela

B. Some Vowel and Consonant Sounds

VOWELS

a like the *a* in *ah, father.*
e like the *a* in *day, ace.*
i like the *i* in *machine, police.*
o like the *o* in *no, note.*
u like the *u* in *rule.*

CONSONANTS

h is never pronounced.
ñ is like *ni* in *onion* or *ny* in *canyon.*
r is pronounced by tapping the tip of the tongue against the gum ridge in back of the upper teeth.
rr is pronounced the same way but rolled, somewhat like the *r* in *three.*
s between vowels is always like *ss* in English *lesson,* never like the *s* (pronounced *z*) in rose.

NOTE:

a. that words ending in a vowel, *n,* or *s* are stressed on the syllable before last:

hora	hour
hablan	they're talking
amigos	friends

b. that all other words are stressed on the last syllable or on the syllable with the accent:

general	general
inglés	English
América	America

LESSON 2

A. COGNATES: WORDS SIMILAR IN ENGLISH AND SPANISH

Now listen to and repeat the following words, which are similar in English and Spanish. These words are descended from the same roots and are called "cognates." Notice how Spanish spelling and pronunciation differ from English:

acción	action	**importante**	important
agente	agent	**interesante**	interesting
atención	attention	**necesario**	necessary
cañón	canyon	**posible**	possible
centro	center	**quieto**	quiet
cheque	check	**radio**	radio
cierto	certain	**restaurante**	restaurant
cuestión	question	**similar**	similar
diferente	different	**té**	tea
difícil	difficult	**teatro**	theater
ejemplo	example	**teléfono**	telephone
gala	gala	**tren**	train
guitarra	guitar	**visita**	visit

B. SPECIAL SOUNDS

1. *c* before *a, o* and *u* is like *k:*

caso   case

2. *c* before *e* and *i* is pronounced in Spain like the *th* in *thin;* in Latin America like the *s* in *see:*

PRONOUNCED AS IN SPAIN	PRONOUNCED AS IN LATIN AMERICA	
cigarro	**cigarro**	cigar
cinco	**cinco**	five

3. *qu* is always followed by *e* or *i* and is pronounced *k*:

quieto   quiet

4. *cc* is always followed by *i*. The first *c* is like *k*, the second is pronounced in Spain like the *th* in *thin* and in Latin America like the *s* in *see*:

PRONOUNCED AS IN SPAIN	PRONOUNCED AS IN LATIN AMERICA	
acción	**acción**	action

5. *cu* is like *qu* in *quick*:

cuestión   question

6. *ch* is like *ch* in *church*:

cheque   check

7. *g* before *a*, *o* and *u* is like *g* in *go*:

gala   gala

8. *g* before *e* and *i* like the *h* in the word *hand*:

general   general

9. *j* is similar to the *h* in *hand:*

ejemplo   example

10. *gu* before *e* and *i* is like *g* in *go*. However, the *u* is not pronounced:

guitarra   guitar

11. *gu* before *a, o* and *u* is like *gw:*

Guatemala   Guatemala

12. Two dots are written over the *u* in the combination *gu* when it is pronounced *gw* before *e* and *i:*

vergüenza   shame

13. *ll* is pronounced like the *y* in *yes:*

millón   million
villa   villa
calle   street

14. *z* is like *c* before *e* and *i:* that is, in Spain it is pronounced like the *th* in *thin* and in Latin America like the *s* in *see:*

PRONOUNCED AS IN SPAIN	PRONOUNCED AS IN LATIN AMERICA	
plaza	**plaza**	plaza, square

LESSON 3

A. The Spanish Alphabet

LETTER	NAME	LETTER	NAME	LETTER	NAME
a	a	j	jota	r	ere
b	be	k	ka	rr	erre
c	ce	l	ele	s	ese
				t	te
d	de	m	eme	u	u
e	e	n	ene	v	ve
f	efe	ñ	eñe	w	doble ve
g	ge	o	o	x	equis
h	hache	p	pe	y	i-griega
i	i	q	cu	z	zeta

NOTE:

a. that the order differs from the order of our alphabet.
b. that *rr* represents a single sound and is treated as one letter (that is, it is never divided).
c. that *ñ* is treated as a separate letter.
d. that the Spanish alphabet has 28 letters—two more than the English.

B. Regional Differences in Pronunciation

The Spanish language is spoken by over 300 million people throughout the world. Slight differences in pronunciation and vocabulary exist between Spain and Latin America. Nonetheless, all speakers understand each other without difficulty. Traditionally, the Spanish spoken in central and northern Spain (Castilian or *castellano*) has been considered a standard throughout the Spanish-speaking world. However, Latin American pronunciation may be more practical for North Americans, who are more frequent visitors to Central and South America than to Spain.

There are a number of minor differences in pronunciation between the various Latin American countries, but like the differences between Castilian and Latin American Spanish, they are not very numerous. The most important regional differences are:

1. *c* before *e* and *i*
   In Spain *th* in *think*. In Latin America *ss* in *lesson*.

2. In Argentina, etc., *ll* and *y* are pronounced like the *s* in measure (at times like the *j* in *judge*).

3. In Puerto Rico, Cuba, Chile, etc., *s* is in some cases completely dropped or is pronounced like an English *h* or a soft Spanish *j* at the end of a syllable:
   esto "this" becomes *e(h)-to*

4. In some regions the *d* in the ending *-ado* is silent:
   comprado "bought" becomes *comprao*

5. In some regions final *n* is pronounced almost like the English *ng* in sing:
   bien "well" is almost *bieng*

[1] You will hear primarily Latin American pronunciation on the tapes that accompany this course. Only lessons 32, 33, 34, and 38 are recorded with the Castilian pronunciation.

LESSON 4

A. VOWELS

The following groups of words will give you some additional practice in Spanish pronunciation and spelling:

  1. *a* is like *ah* or the *a* in *father:*

a	to, at	**las**	the *(fem. pl.)*[1]
amigo	friend	**pan**	bread
la	the *(fem. s.)*[1]	**habla**	he *(or* she) is speaking

  2. *e* is like the *ay* in *day* but cut off sharply:

el	the	**carne**	meat
de	of	**tren**	train
en	in	**tres**	three
padre	father	**este**	this
se	itself		

Notice that when *e* comes at the end of a word or syllable it is close to the *ay* in *day* (but cut off sharply). Otherwise it is closer to our *e* in *ten*.

  3. *i* is like the *i* in *police, machine, marine:*

mí	me	**hijo**	son
sí	yes	**muy**	very
amiga	friend *(fem.)*	**hoy**	today

---

[1] All nouns in Spanish are either masculine or feminine, and the words that modify them usually indicate their gender and number. In this book, feminine is abbreviated to *fem.*, masculine to *masc.*, singular to *s.*, and plural to *pl.*

When it follows a vowel or stands by itself, *y* is pronounced like the Spanish *i: muy* "very," *y* "and." Otherwise it is like English *y: yo* "I."

4. *o* is like the *o* in *no:*

no	no	**ocho**	eight
dos	two	**pequeño**	small
hora	hour	**febrero**	February
con	with		

Notice that when *o* comes at the end of a word or syllable it sounds like the *o* in *no* (but cut off sharply). Otherwise it is closer to the *o* in *north.*

5. *u* is like the *u* in *rule:*

uno	one *(masc.)*	**tú**	you *(familiar)*[2]
una	one *(fem.)*	**mucho**	much

6. Notice that each vowel is clearly pronounced. Vowels are not slurred over as they often are in English:

rápido	quick	**idea**	idea
leer	to read	**peor**	worse
parte	he leaves	**día**	day
ahí	there	**mío**	mine
puro	pure	**país**	country

---

[2] Spanish has both familiar and polite forms of *you.* The familar *tú* is used when speaking to friends, family and children. See Lesson 9 for more information.

B. Diphthongs (Common Vowel Pairs)

1. *ai, ay*

aire	air	**hay**	there is, there are

2. *au*

restaurante	restaurant	**automóvil**	automobile
autobús	bus		

3. *ei, ey*

seis	six	**ley**	law
treinta	thirty		

4. *ia, ya*

gracias	thanks	**estudiar**	to study
comercial	commercial	**ya**	already

5. *ie, ye*

pie	foot	**bien**	well
siete	seven	**quién**	who
quiero	I want	**cien**	hundred
tiene	he has	**siempre**	always
diez	ten	**yerba**	grass

6. *io, yo*

despacio	slowly	**acción**	action
estación	station	**yo**	I

7. *iu, yu*

ciudad	city	**yuca**	yucca plant

8. *oi, oy*

estoy	I am	**voy**	I'm going
hoy	today	**oiga**	listen

9. *ua*

Juan	John	**¿Cuánto?**	How much?
¿Cuál?	Which?	**cuatro**	four

10. *ue*

nueve	nine	**puerta**	door
fuego	fire		

11. *uo*

continuo	continuous	**antiguo**	old

12. *ui, uy*

muy	very	**ruido**	noise
¡Cuidado!	Careful!		

LESSON 5

A. CONSONANTS

1. *b* and *v:* Most Spanish speakers pronounce both letters alike. At the beginning of a word and after *m* or *n* they pronounce both *b* and *v* like English *b:*

bueno	good	**veinte**	twenty
vaso	glass	**hombre**	man

When *b* and *v* come between vowels they pronounce them somewhat like English *v:*

Cuba	Cuba	**haber**	to have
La Habana	Havana		

The sound differs from our *v* in that, instead of bringing the lower lip against the upper teeth, you bring the two lips together, the way you do when blowing dust from something.

However, some Spanish speakers pronounce *b* and *v* the way we do in English: they pronounce *b* whenever a *b* occurs in the spelling and *v* whenever a *v* occurs in the spelling:

vivir	to live	**beber**	to drink

2. *c* before consonants and the vowels *a, o,* and *u* is pronounced *k:*

cosa	thing	**cuánto**	how much
casa	house		

—before *e* and *i* it is pronounced in Spain like the *th* in *thin* and in Latin America like the *s* in *see:*

cerca	near	**fácil**	easy
servicio	service	**docena**	dozen
cierto	certain		

3. *ch* is as in *church:*

mucho	much	**noche**	night
ocho	eight		

4. *d* is like the English *d* except that the tip of the tongue touches the back of the upper teeth. After a pause or after *n* it is pronounced like *d* in *day:*

día	day	**donde**	where
cúando	when		

—between vowels it is pronounced like *th* in *then:*

nada	nothing	**poder**	to be able
todo	all		

5. *f* is as in English:

familia   family

6. *g* before a consonant is like the *g* in *go:*

grande   big, large

—before *a, o* and *u* it is like *g* in *go:*

lugar	place	**gusto**	pleasure

—before *e* and *i* it is like the Spanish *j* (a strong rasping *h*, somewhat like the sound you make when you clear your throat):

general	general	**Gibraltar**	Gibraltar

—*gü* is like *gw:*

vergüenza   shame

7. *h* is never pronounced:

ahora   now   **hablo**   I speak

8. *j* is a strong *h* (the same sound as *g* before *e* and *i*):

julio   July   **mejor**   better
jabón   soap

9. *ll* is pronounced like the *y* in *yes:*

Me llamo . . .   My name is . . .
pollo   chicken

10. *m* is as in English:

mismo   the same

11. *n* is as in English:

nunca   never

12. *ñ* is like the *ni* in *onion* or the *ny* in *canyon:*

español   Spanish   **mañana**   tomorrow

13. *p* is as in English:

para   for

14. *qu* is like the English *k:*

¿Qué?   What?

15. *r* is made by tapping the tip of the tongue against the gum ridge back of the upper teeth, somewhat like British "veddy" for "very":

América   America

16. *rr* is made by trilling the tip of the tongue against the gum ridge back of the upper teeth, like the *r* in *three:*

cigarrillo   cigarette

When *r* comes at the beginning of a word it is pronounced like *rr:*

rico   rich

Listen to the following words, the first of which has *r,* the second *rr:*

pero	but	**perro**	dog
caro	dear; expensive	**carro**	car; cart

17. *s* is like the *s* in *see* or the *ss* in *lesson* (never as in *rose*):

casa   house

18. *t* is as in English except that the tip of the tongue touches the back of the upper teeth:

fruta   fruit

19. *y* is as in yes:

ayer   yesterday

y meaning "and" is pronounced like *i* (see page 9):

norte y sur   north and south

20. *z* is like *c* before *e* and *i;* that is, it is pronounced in Spain like the *th* in *thin* and in Latin America like the *s* in *see:*

PRONOUNCED AS IN SPAIN	PRONOUNCED AS IN LATIN AMERICA	
diez	diez	ten
voz	voz	voice
luz	luz	light
marzo	marzo	March
azul	azul	blue
razón	razón	reason

B.   MORE ENGLISH-SPANISH COGNATES

Building up a Spanish vocabulary is a rather easy matter since there are a great number of English cognates. Many words are spelled exactly the same (though they may differ considerably in pronunciation):

SPANISH	ENGLISH	SPANISH	ENGLISH
actor	actor	familiar	familiar
animal	animal	gas	gas
auto	auto	general	general
capital	capital	hospital	hospital
central	central	hotel	hotel
chocolate	chocolate	humor	humor
color	color	idea	idea
doctor	doctor	local	local

motor	motor	**similar**	similar
original	original	**simple**	simple
personal	personal	**terrible**	terrible
probable	probable	**total**	total
regular	regular	**usual**	usual

There are many Spanish words which you will have no difficulty in recognizing despite minor differences. Some of these differences are:

1. The Spanish word has an accent mark:

área	area	*melón*	melon
conclusión	conclusion	*ómnibus*	omnibus
cónsul	consul	*religión*	religion

2. The Spanish word has a single consonant:

antena	antenna	*inteligente*	intelligent
anual	annual	*ocasional*	occasional
comercial	commercial	*oficial*	official
imposible	impossible	*posible*	possible
intelectual	intellectual	*profesional*	professional

3. The Spanish word adds *-a*, *-e*, or *-o:*

lista	list	*parte*	part
mapa	map	*líquido*	liquid
problema	problem	*portero*	porter
persona	person	*producto*	product
costo	cost	*restaurante*	restaurant

4. The Spanish word ends in *a* or *o,* the English word in *e:*

causa	cause	*estado*	state
figura	figure	*estilo*	style
medicina	medicine	*favorito*	favorite

nota	note	*minuto*	minute
práctica	practice	*tubo*	tube
rosa	rose	*uso*	use

5. The Spanish word is slightly different in other respects:

| *automóvil* | automobile | *especial* | special |
| *cuestión* | question | *origen* | origin |

C. GENERAL SPELLING EQUIVALENTS

1. Spanish *c (qu)* = English *k (ck):*

| *franco* | frank | *parque* | park |
| *saco* | sack | *ataque* | attack |

2. Spanish *f* = English *ph:*

| *frase* | phrase, sentence | *físico* | physical |
| | | *teléfono* | telephone |

3. Spanish *j* = English *x:*

| *ejecutar* | to execute | *ejemplo* | example |
| *ejercicio* | exercise | *fijar* | fix |

4. Spanish *t* = English *th:*

autor	author	*teatro*	theatre
autoridad	authority	*teoría*	theory
simpatía	sympathy		

5. Spanish *z* = English *ce:*

| *comenzar* | commence | *raza* | race |
| *fuerza* | force | | |

6. Spanish *i* = English *y:*

estilo	style	*sistema*	system
misterio	mystery	*ritmo*	rhythm

7. Spanish *o* and *u* = English *ou:*

hora	hour	*sonido*	sound
corte	court	*sopa*	soup
montaña	mountain	*fundar*	found
anunciar	announce	*curso*	course

8. Spanish *ia* and *io* = English *y:*

compañía	company	*secretaria*	secretary
familia	family	*remedio*	remedy
historia	history	*territorio*	territory

9. Spanish *ia* and *io* = English *e:*

ausencia	absence	*policía*	police
diferencia	difference	*comercio*	commerce
distancia	distance	*edificio*	edifice,
experiencia	experience		building
noticia	notice	*silencio*	silence
justicia	justice	*servicio*	service

10. Spanish *ción* = English *tion:*

acción	action	*conversación*	conversation
atracción	attraction	*descripción*	description
estación	station	*satisfacción*	satisfaction
información	information	*sensación*	sensation

11. Spanish *o* = English *al:*

eléctrico	electric(al)	*político*	political
eterno	eternal	*práctico*	practical

12. Spanish *oso* = English *ous:*

| *delicioso* | delicious | *numeroso* | numerous |
| *famoso* | famous | *religioso* | religious |

LESSON 6

A. Days and Months[1]

lunes	Monday
martes	Tuesday
miércoles	Wednesday
jueves	Thursday
viernes	Friday
sábado	Saturday
domingo	Sunday

enero	January
febrero	February
marzo	March
abril	April
mayo	May
junio	June
julio	July
agosto	August
septiembre	September
octubre	October
noviembre	November
diciembre	December

[1] Note that the days of the week and the months of the year are not capitalized in Spanish.

B. Numbers 1–10

uno	one
dos	two
tres	three
cuatro	four
cinco	five
seis	six
siete	seven
ocho	eight
nueve	nine
diez	ten
Uno y uno son dos.	One and one are two.
Uno y dos son tres.	One and two are three.
Dos y dos son cuatro.	Two and two are four.
Dos y tres son cinco.	Two and three are five.
Tres y tres son seis.	Three and three are six
Tres y cuatro son siete.	Three and four are seven.
Cuatro y cuatro son ocho.	Four and four are eight.
Cuatro y cinco son nueve.	Four and five are nine.
Cinco y cinco son diez.	Five and five are ten.

C. Colors

rojo	red
azul	blue
verde	green
negro	black
blanco	white
amarillo	yellow
café	brown (coffee color)
castaño	brown (chestnut color)
gris	gray

D. Seasons and Directions

la primavera	spring
el verano	summer
el otoño	autumn
el invierno	winter
norte	north
sur	south
este	east
oeste	west

E. Morning, Noon and Night; Today, Yesterday, Tomorrow

mañana	morning
mediodía	noon
tarde	afternoon
noche	evening, night
hoy	today
ayer	yesterday
mañana	tomorrow
Hoy es viernes.	Today is Friday.
Ayer fue jueves.	Yesterday was Thursday.
Mañana es sábado.	Tomorrow is Saturday.

QUIZ 1

Try matching these two columns:

1. *viernes*   a. January
2. *otoño*   b. summer
3. *jueves*   c. June
4. *primavera*   d. winter

5. *ocho*	e. October
6. *enero*	f. white
7. *invierno*	g. autumn
8. *verde*	h. Sunday
9. *junio*	i. eight
10. *verano*	j. spring
11. *lunes*	k. west
12. *cuatro*	l. Thursday
13. *octubre*	m. four
14. *domingo*	n. ten
15. *oeste*	o. red
16. *rojo*	p. black
17. *negro*	q. green
18. *diez*	r. Friday
19. *blanco*	s. gray
20. *gris*	t. Monday

ANSWERS
1—r; 2—g; 3—l; 4—j; 5—i; 6—a; 7—d; 8—q; 9—c;
10—b; 11—t; 12—m; 13—e; 14—h; 15—k; 16—o;
17—p; 18—n; 19—f; 20—s.

F. WORD STUDY

clase	class
considerable	considerable
diferencia	difference
elemento	element
gloria	glory
operación	operation
madre	mother
padre	father

LESSON 7

A. Greetings

POR LA MAÑANA	IN THE MORNING
buenos	good *(masc. pl.)*
días	day ("days")
Buenos días	Good morning.
señor	Mr.
García	García
Buenos días, señor García.	Good morning, Mr. García.
cómo	how
está	are
usted	you
¿Cómo está usted?	How are you *(pol.)?*[1]
	How do you do?
cómo	how
estás	are
tú	you *(fam.)*[1]
¿Cómo estás?	How are you *(fam.)*?
muy	very
bien	well
Muy bien.	Very well.
gracias	thank you, thanks
Muy bien, gracias.	Very well, thank you.
y	and
usted	you
¿Y usted?	And how are you *(pol.)?* ("And you?")
¿Y tú?	And how are you *(fam.)?* ("And you?")
bien	fine
Bien, gracias.	Fine, thank you.

[1] In this book, *pol.* stands for "polite," and *fam.* stands for "familiar." For more information, see Lesson 8.

POR LA TARDE	IN THE AFTERNOON
buenas	good *(fem. pl.)*
tardes	afternoon ("afternoons")
Buenas tardes.	Good afternoon.
Buenas tardes, señora García.	Good afternoon, Mrs. García.
muy	very
buenas	good
tardes	afternoon
Muy buenas tardes, señor López.	Good afternoon, Mr. López.
cómo	how
se encuentra	find yourself
usted	you
¿Cómo se encuentra usted?	How are you?
Más o menos	So-so ("more or less")
Más o menos, ¿y usted?	So-so, and how are you?
pues	as
aquí	here
estamos	we are
Pues aquí estamos, gracias.	Same as usual, thanks.

AL ANOCHECER	IN THE EVENING
Y DE NOCHE	AND AT NIGHT
buenas	good
noches	evening ("nights")
Buenas noches, señorita Quintana.	Good evening (Good night), Miss Quintana.
muy	very
buenas	good

| **Muy buenas Don Pedro.**[1] | Good evening (Good night), Don Pedro. |
| **Muy buenas Doña Ana.** | Good evening (Good night), Doña Ana. |

EN CUALQUIER MOMENTO DEL DIA	AT ANY TIME OF DAY
Hola.	Hello. Hi.
Adiós.	Good-bye.

Note: *Señor* (sir, mister) and *Señora* (madam, Mrs.) are general terms of address. *Don* and *Doña* are primarily used only with a person's first name and imply both respect and a certain degree of familiarity. In formal situations, *Don* and *Doña* are used with complete names: Don Pedro García de la Vega, Doña Ana Cárdenas de Menezes.

B. How's the Weather?

¿Qué tiempo hace?	How's the weather? What's the weather like?
Hace frío.	It's cold.
Hace calor.	It's hot.
Hace buen tiempo.	It's nice.
Hace viento.	It's windy.
Hace sol.	It's sunny.
Llueve.	It's raining.
Nieva.	It's snowing.
¡Vaya calor!	What heat!
Llueve a cántaros.	It's raining cats and dogs.

[1] *Muy buenas* is a popular way to say "Good evening" or "Good night" in colloquial speech.

QUIZ 2

1. *mañana*	a. Good afternoon.
2. *señora*	b. How are you?
3. *¿Cómo está usted?*	c. What's the weather like?
4. *Muy bien.*	d. morning
5. *Buenos días.*	e. Thank you.
6. *Muy buenas noches.*	f. Madam or Mrs.
7. *¿Cómo se encuentra usted?*	g. It's hot.
8. *Aquí estamos.*	h. Sir or Mr.
9. *Gracias.*	i. How?
10. *Hace calor.*	j. Good morning.
11. *¿Qué tiempo hace?*	k. in the evening.
12. *Buenas tardes.*	l. How are you?
13. *¿Cómo?*	m. Very well.
14. *señor*	n. Same as usual.
15. *al anochecer*	o. Good evening. (Good night).

ANSWERS

1—d; 2—f; 3—l; 4—m; 5—j; 6—o; 7—b; 8—n;
9—e; 10—g; 11—c; 12—a; 13—i; 14—h; 15—k.

LESSON 8

A. WHERE IS . . . ?

dónde	where
hay	there is, are
¿Dónde hay . . . ?	Where is there . . . ?
un	a
hotel	hotel

¿Dónde hay un hotel?	Where's there a hotel?
buen	good
restaurante[1]	restaurant
¿Dónde hay un buen restaurante?	Where's there a good restaurant?
dónde	where
está	is
¿Dónde está?	Where is (it)?
¿Dónde está el teléfono?	Where's the telephone?
¿Dónde está el restaurante?	Where's the restaurant?
¿Dónde está la estación del tren?	Where's the train station?
¿Dónde está el aeropuerto?	Where's the airport?
¿Dónde está el baño?	Where is the bathroom?

B. CAN YOU TELL ME . . . ?

puede usted	can you
decirme	tell me
¿Puede usted decirme . . . ?	Can you tell me . . . ?
¿Puede usted decirme dónde hay un hotel?	Can you tell me where there is a hotel?
¿Puede usted decirme dónde hay un buen restaurante?	Can you tell me where there is a good restaurant?
¿Puede usted decirme dónde está el teléfono?	Can you tell me where the telephone is?

[1] There are two common spellings and pronunciations: *restaurante* and *restorán*.

¿Puede usted decirme dónde está la estación del tren?	Can you tell me where the train station is?
¿Puede usted decirme dónde está el aeropuerto?	Can you tell me where the airport is?

QUIZ 3

1.	*¿Dónde hay un hotel?*	a. Where's the telephone?
2.	*¿Dónde está el teléfono?*	b. Can you tell me where the train station is?
3.	*¿Puede usted decirme . . . ?*	c. Can you tell me . . . ?
4.	*¿Puede usted decirme dónde está la estación del tren?*	d. the airport
5.	*el aeropuerto*	e. Where is there a hotel?

ANSWERS
1—e; 2—a; 3—c; 4—b; 5—d.

C. DO YOU HAVE . . . ?

¿Tiene usted . . . ?	Do you have . . . ?
dinero	(any) money
cigarrillos	(any) cigarettes
fósforos	(any) matches
un carro	a car
Necesito . . .	I need . . .
papel	(some) paper

lápiz	(a) pencil
bolígrafo	pen
un sello de correo	a postage stamp
jabón	soap
pasta dentífrica	toothpaste
una toalla	a towel
¿Dónde puedo comprar . . . ?	Where can I buy . . . ?
un diccionario de español	a Spanish dictionary
una guía turística	a tourist guidebook
unos libros en inglés	some books in English
ropa	(some) clothes

D. IN A RESTAURANT

desayuno	breakfast
almuerzo	lunch
comida	dinner
cena	supper
¿Qué desea usted?	What will you have? ("What do you wish?")
deme	give me
el menú	the menu
por favor	please
Deme el menú, por favor.	May I have a menu, please?
Tráigame . . .	Bring me . . .
un poco de pan	(some) bread
pan y mantequilla	bread and butter
sopa	soup
carne	meat

carne de res	beef
biftec	steak
jamón	ham
pescado	fish
pollo	chicken
huevos	eggs
legumbres	vegetables
patatas	potatoes
ensalada	salad
agua mineral	mineral water
vino	wine
cerveza	beer
leche	milk
café con leche	coffee with milk
azúcar	sugar
sal	salt
pimienta	pepper
fruta	fruit
postre	dessert

Tráigame . . .	Bring me . . .
una taza de café	a cup of coffee
una taza de té	a cup of tea
una servilleta	a napkin
una cuchara	a spoon
una cucharita[1]	a teaspoon
una cucharilla[1]	a teaspoon
un cuchillo	a knife
un plato	a plate
un vaso	a glass

Quisiera . . .	I would like . . .
un poco de fruta	some fruit
una botella de vino	a bottle of wine

[1] *Cucharilla* is the more common word in Spain, *cucharita* the more common word in Latin America.

una botella de vino tinto	a bottle of red wine
una botella de vino blanco	a bottle of white wine
otra botella de vino	another bottle of wine
un poco más de eso	a little more of that
un poco más de pan	a little more bread
un poco más de carne	a little more meat
La cuenta, por favor.	The check, please.

QUIZ 4

1. *carne*
2. *patatas*
3. *agua*
4. *¿Qué desea usted?*
5. *huevos*
6. *pollo*
7. *pescado*
8. *una botella de vino*
9. *Necesito jabón.*
10. *Tráigame un poco de pan.*
11. *café con leche*
12. *azúcar*
13. *legumbres*
14. *una taza de té*
15. *un poco más de pan*
16. *un cuchillo*
17. *postre*

a. fish
b. water
c. vegetables
d. I need soap.
e. The check, please.
f. breakfast
g. a spoon
h. coffee with milk
i. What will you have?
j. dessert
k. meat
l. a knife
m. eggs
n. Bring me some bread.
o. chicken
p. a cup of tea
q. some more bread

18. *desayuno*   r. sugar
19. *una cuchara*   s. a bottle of wine
20. *La cuenta, por favor.*   t. potatoes

ANSWERS
1—k; 2—t; 3—b; 4—i; 5—m; 6—o; 7—a; 8—s;
9—d; 10—n; 11—h; 12—r; 13—c; 14—p; 15—q;
16—l; 17—j; 18—f; 19—g; 20—e.

LESSON 9

This lesson and several of the following lessons are
longer than the others. They contain the grammatical
information you need to know from the start. Read each
section until you understand every point; as you continue with the course, try to observe examples of the
points mentioned. Refer back to the grammatical sections as often as necessary. In this way you will eventu-
ally find that you have a good grasp of the basic features
of Spanish grammar without any deliberate memoriz-
ing of "rules." Be sure to refer to the Summary of
Spanish Grammar (beginning on page 243), as well.

A. TO SPEAK: *HABLAR*

1. I speak

yo hablo   I speak
tú hablas   you speak *(fam.)*
él habla   he speaks
ella habla   she speaks

| usted habla | you speak *(pol.)* |
| nosotros hablamos | we speak *(masc.)* |

nosotras hablamos	we speak *(fem.)*
vosotros habláis	you speak *(masc.)*
vosotras habláis	you speak *(fem.)*
ellos hablan	they speak *(masc.)*
ellas hablan	they speak *(fem.)*
ustedes hablan	you speak *(pol.)*

2. Study these examples:

Hablo español.	I speak Spanish.
Juan habla inglés.	Juan speaks English.
Elena y yo hablamos español.	Elena and I speak Spanish.

NOTE:

a. These forms, which make up the present tense, translate English "I speak," "I am speaking," "I do speak."

b. *Tú* "you" is used to address people you know very well (whom you call by first name in English—relatives, close friends, etc.) and to address children, pets, etc. The plural of *tú* is *vosotros* (fem. *vosotras*), which is used in Spain. In Latin America the plural form for "you" *ustedes* is used even with close friends. *Tú* is called the "familiar" form, *usted* the "polite" or "formal."

3. Notice that there are six verb endings:

SINGULAR

-o   indicates the speaker (I).

-as   indicates the person spoken to (you). It is
            only used to address someone you know
            well.

-a   indicates someone or something spoken
            about (he, she, it) or else you *(polite)*.

PLURAL

-amos   indicates several people (we).

-áis   indicates the persons spoken to (you). It is
            used in Spain to address only those peo-
            ple you know well.

-an   indicates they (both masculine and femi-
            nine) or you *(polite* in Spain).

These are the forms for verbs with the infinitive
ending *-ar*. Other common *-ar* verbs are:

trabajar   to work
viajar   to travel

Later on you will study the forms of regular verbs with
infinitive endings *-er* and *-ir*.

4. Notice that the verb form with *usted, él,* and *ella*
   is the same: *habla*.

5. The pronouns *yo, tú, él, ella,* etc. are not ordinarily used. "I speak" is just *hablo,* "we speak"
   is *hablamos,* the *-o* and *-amos* being sufficient to
   indicate "I," and "we." The pronouns are used
   only for emphasis or clarity (i.e., *usted habla*
   "you speak" and *él habla* "he speaks").

6. Notice that several forms of the pronouns differ depending on whether men or women are speaking.

él habla	he is speaking
ella habla	she is speaking
nosotros hablamos	we are speaking *(men)*
nosotras hablamos	we are speaking *(women)*
vosotros habláis	you *(fam.)* are speaking *(men)*
vosotras habláis	you *(fam.)* are speaking *(women)*
ellos hablan	they are speaking *(men)*
ellas hablan	they are speaking *(women)*

7. *Usted* (abbreviated *Ud.*[1]) and *ustedes* (*Uds.*) are abbreviations of *vuestra merced*, "Your Grace" (plural: *vuestras mercedes*) and therefore take the third person form: *¿Cómo está usted?*

B. THE AND A[2]

1. The

el muchacho	the boy	**los muchachos**	the boys
la muchacha	the girl	**las muchachas**	the girls

Notice that the word for "the" is in some cases *el* (plural: *los*), in other cases *la* (plural: *las*). Nouns that take *el* are called "masculine,"

---

[1] The abbreviation *Ud. (Uds.)* is used in Latin America; in Spain the form *Vd. (Vds.)* is also used.
[2] Be sure to check the Summary of Spanish Grammar for more information for sections B–G.

nouns that take *la* are called "feminine." Nouns referring to males are masculine, nouns referring to females are feminine. In the case of other nouns you have to learn whether the noun is masculine (that is, takes *el*) or feminine (that is, takes *la*).

Lo "the" is used before parts of speech other than nouns when they are used as nouns:

lo importante	important thing
lo necesario	the necessary thing
lo dicho	what is said

2. A (An)

un muchacho	a boy
una muchacha	a girl
unos muchachos	boys, some (a few) boys
unas muchachas	girls, some (a few) girls

Unos (unas) is often used when we would use "some" or "a few" in English: *unos días,* "a few days."

QUIZ 5

1. *yo*	a. they speak
2. *nosotros*	b. she is speaking
3. *usted habla*	c. she
4. *él*	d. you *(fam. plural)*
5. *ellos hablan*	e. I
6. *vosotros*	f. you speak
7. *tú*	g. he

8. *ella*   h. we speak *(women)*
9. *nosotras hablamos*   i. you *(fam. sing.)*
10. *ella habla*   j. we

ANSWERS
1—e; 2—j; 3—f; 4—g; 5—a; 6—d; 7—i; 8—c; 9—h;
10—b.

C. CONTRACTIONS

de + el = del   of the, from the
a + el = al   to the
del muchacho   of (from) the boy
al muchacho   to the boy

D. PLURALS

1. To form the plural of a noun ending in a vowel
   you add *-s:*

el libro   the book   **los libros**   the books
la carta   the letter   **las cartas**   the letters

2. If the noun ends in a consonant you add *-es:*

la mujer   the woman   **las mujeres**   the women

3. If the noun ends in *-z* you change the *z* to *c* and
   then add *-es:*

la luz   the light   **las luces**   the lights

E. ADJECTIVES

un muchacho alto	a tall boy
una muchacha alta	a tall girl
unos muchachos altos	tall boys, some (a few) tall boys
unas muchachas altas	tall girls, some (a few) tall girls

Adjectives generally follow the noun and have the same form (that is, masculine if the noun is masculine, plural if the noun is plural, etc.).

When an adjective is used by itself, its form tells you whether the reference is to men (or masculine nouns) or to women (or feminine nouns) and whether it is to one person (or thing) or to several:

(él) Es español.	He's Spanish.
(ella) Es española.	She's Spanish.
(ellos) Son españoles.	They're Spanish *(masc.).*
(ellas) Son españolas.	They're Spanish *(fem.).*

F. POSSESSIVE "DE"

English *-'s* or *-s'* is translated by *de* "of":

el libro de Juan	John's book ("the book of John")
los libros de los muchachos	the boys' books ("the books of the boys")

G. ASKING A QUESTION

1. To ask a question you put the subject after the verb:

Usted habla español. You speak Spanish.
¿Habla usted español? Do you speak Spanish?

2. In popular speech you can also ask a question by using the same sentence order as for a statement and raising the tone of your voice at the end.

Usted habla español. You speak Spanish.
¿Usted habla español? Do you speak Spanish?

3. Adjectives come right after the verb:

¿Es fácil el español? Is Spanish easy?

H. NOT

The word for "not" is *no*. It comes before the verb:

No hablo inglés. I don't speak English.

REVIEW QUIZ 1

1. *Buenas_____ (afternoon), señora García.*
   a. *mañana*
   b. *tardes*
   c. *gracias*

2. *¿Puede usted decirme_____ (where) está el correo?*
   a. *dónde*
   b. *buen*
   c. *allá*

3. _____ (bring me) *un poco de pan.*
   a. *desea*
   b. *tomar*
   c. *tráigame*

4. *Café con*_____ (milk), *por favor.*
   a. *azúcar*
   b. *vino*
   c. *leche*

5. *Un poco*_____ (more) *de carne.*
   a. *más*
   b. *taza*
   c. *otra*

6. *El siete de*_____ (January).
   a. *marzo*
   b. *enero*
   c. *agosto*

7. _____ (Wednesday), *el cinco de septiembre.*
   a. *viernes*
   b. *sábado*
   c. *miércoles*

8. ¿_____ (how) *está usted?*
   a. *gracias*
   b. *cómo*
   c. *tardes*

9. *La Señorita García*_____ (speaks) *español.*
   a. *hablo*
   b. *habla*
   c. *hablan*

10. *Quisiera una botella de_____* (wine).
    a. *leche*
    b. *vino*
    c. *agua*

ANSWERS
1—b; 2—a; 3—c; 4—c; 5—a; 6—b; 7—c; 8—b;
9—b; 10—b.

LESSON 10

A. MAY I INTRODUCE . . . ?

Buenos días.	Good morning.
Buenos días, señor.	Good morning (sir).
¿Cómo está usted?	How are you?
Muy bien, gracias. ¿Y usted?	Very well, thanks. How are you?
¿Es usted norteamericano?	Are you from the United States?
Sí, señor.	Yes (sir).
¿Habla usted español?	Do you speak Spanish?
Un poco.	A little.
le presento	I present you
a mi amiga	to my friend
la Señorita Gallego	Miss Gallego
Le presento a mi amiga, la Señorita Gallego.	May I introduce my friend, Miss Gallego?
mucho gusto	much pleasure
en conocerla	in meeting you

Mucho gusto en conocerla.	I'm glad to meet you.
Mucho gusto.	It's nice to meet you. A pleasure.
el gusto	the pleasure
es mío	is mine
El gusto es mío.	The pleasure is mine.
permita usted	permit me
que me presente	to (that I) introduce myself
soy José Barrio	I'm Jose Barrio
para servirle	at your service ("to serve you")

Permita usted que me presente; soy José Barrio, para servirle.	May I introduce myself? I'm Jose Barrio.
Manuel Fernández a sus órdenes	Manuel Fernández at your service ("at your orders")
Manuel Fernández, a sus órdenes.	I'm Manuel Fernández.
permítame	allow me
presentarle	to introduce you
a mi amigo	to my friend
Permítame presentarle a mi amigo el doctor Pérez.	Allow me to introduce you to my friend Dr. Pérez.
tanto	so much
gusto	pleasure
en	in
conocerlo	meeting you

Tanto gusto en conocerlo[1], Dr. Pérez.	It's such a pleasure to meet you, Dr. Pérez.
el gusto	the pleasure
es mío	is mine
El gusto es mío, señor.	The pleasure is mine, sir.
he tenido	I've had
un verdadero	a real
gusto	pleasure
He tenido un verdadero gusto.	It's been a real pleasure.
el gusto	the pleasure
ha sido mío	has been mine.
El gusto ha sido mío.	The pleasure has been mine.

B. How Are Things?

¡Hola, Manuel!	Hello, Manuel.
¡Hola, Betina!	Hello, Betina.
¡Dichosos los ojos!	It's nice to see you! ("Fortunate eyes!")
¿Como estás?	How are you?
¿Qué tal?	How are things? How are you?
Bien, ¿y tú?	Okay, and how are you?
qué	what
hay	is there

[1] Notice that you say *conocerla* when speaking to a woman and *conocerlo* when speaking to a man. In Spain, you will hear *conocerle* for a man or a woman.

de	of
nuevo	new
¿Qué hay de nuevo?	What's new?

nada	nothing
de	in
particular	particular
Nada de particular.	Nothing in particular.
qué	what
me cuenta	do (you) tell me
usted	you
¿Qué hubo?	What's up?
¿Qué me cuenta usted?	What's new?
poca	little
cosa	thing
Poca cosa.	Not much.

C. GOOD-BYE

Adiós.	Good-bye.
hasta	until
otro	another
día	day
Hasta otro día	See you soon. ("Until another day.")
Adiós. Hasta otro día.	Good-bye. See you soon.

hasta	until
luego	later
Hasta luego.	See you later.
hasta	until
la vista	the sight
Hasta la vista.	See you soon. So long.

Buenas noches.	Good night. Good evening.
muy	very
buenas	good
Muy buenas.	Good night. Good evening.
Hasta mañana.	See you tomorrow.

QUIZ 6

1. *¿Qué tal?*	a. Nothing in particular.
2. *Hasta luego.*	b. Allow me to introduce you to my friend.
3. *Buenas noches.*	c. See you later.
4. *Hola Juan.*	d. Hello, John.
5. *Nada de particular.*	e. It's nice to meet you.
6. *Permítame presentarle a mi amigo.*	f. How are you?
7. *Hasta la vista.*	g. Good night.
8. *nuevo*	h. to know you
9. *Mucho gusto.*	i. new
10. *conocerlo*	j. So long.

ANSWERS
1—f; 2—j; 3—g; 4—d; 5—a; 6—b; 7—c; 8—i; 9—e; 10—h.

LESSON 11

A. TO BE OR NOT TO BE: *SER, ESTAR*

There are two verbs in Spanish for "to be": *ser* and *estar*. In general *ser* indicates an inherent characteristic (e.g., I'm an American) and is also used to state professions while *estar* indicates a location, condition, or state (e.g., I'm tired).

1. SER

yo soy	I am
tú eres	you are
él[1] es	he is
nosotros somos	we are
vosotros sois	you are
ellos[1] son	they are

2. ESTAR

yo estoy	I am
tú estás	you are
él está	he is
nosotros estamos	we are
vosotros estáis	you are
ellos están	they are

3. Study these phrases with *ser* and *estar*. Note the different uses as explained above.

SER

El es médico.	He's a doctor.
Es español.	He's a Spaniard. He's Spanish.
Ella es joven.	She's young.
Es inteligente.	She's intelligent.
Soy yo.	It's me (I).
¿De dónde es usted?	Where are you from?
Soy de España.	I'm from Spain.

---

[1] *Él* will represent the singular third-person forms *(él, ella, usted)* and *ellos* will represent the plural third-person forms *(ellos, ellas, ustedes.)*

¿Es de madera?	Is it made of wood?
¿De quién es esto?	Whose is this?
Esto es de él.	This is his.
Es la una.	It's one o'clock.
Es necesario.	It's necessary.

ESTAR

Está allí.	He's over there.
Está en México.[1]	He's in Mexico.
¿Dónde está el libro?	Where's the book?
Está sobre la mesa.	It's on the table.
Estoy cansado.	I'm tired.
Estoy listo.	I'm ready.
El café está frío.	The coffee is cold.
Está claro.	It's clear. It's obvious.
La ventana está abierta.	The window is open.
La ventana está cerrada.	The window is shut.

NOTE:

Adjectives used with *ser* and *estar* must agree with the subject in gender and number, according to the rules explained in Lesson 8, item E.

Ella es española.	She's Spanish.
Ellos son cubanos.	They're Cuban.
Ella está cansada.	She's tired.

See pages 307–311 of the Summary of Spanish Grammar for more information.

---

[1] In the word *México* the *x* is pronounced as though it were written *j*.

QUIZ 7

1. *Es inteligente.*	a. Whose is this?
2. *Es una lástima.*	b. Where are you from?
3. *El es médico.*	c. they are
4. *Yo soy*	d. He's a doctor.
5. *Es la una.*	e. It's me.
6. *nosotros somos*	f. He's a Spaniard.
7. *Es de madera.*	g. He's intelligent.
8. *¿De dónde es usted?*	h. It's a pity.
9. *Está allí.*	i. I am.
10. *Soy yo.*	j. It's one o'clock.
11. *Estoy cansado.*	k. It's made of wood.
12. *ellos están*	l. we are
13. *¿De quién es esto?*	m. He's over there.
14. *Es necesario.*	n. I'm tired.
15. *Es español.*	o. It's necessary.

ANSWERS

1—g; 2—h; 3—d; 4—i; 5—j; 6—l; 7—k; 8—b; 9—m; 10—e; 11—n; 12—c; 13—a; 14—o; 15—f.

B. IT IS

Es ...	It is ...
Es verdad.	It's true.
Eso no es verdad.	That isn't true. That isn't so.
Es así.	It's so. That's the way it is.
Es cierto.	It's certain.
Es grande.	It's big.
Es pequeño.	It's small.
Es caro.	It's expensive.

Es barato.	It's cheap.
Es de pacotilla *(fam.)*.	It's worthless. It's junk.
Es bobo *(fam.)*.	It's silly. It's stupid.
Es difícil.	It's difficult.
Es fácil.	It's easy.
¡Es pan comido!	It's easy! ("It's eaten bread!")
Es poco.	It's a little. It's not much.
Es muy poco.	It's very little.
Es mucho.	It's a lot.
Es bastante.	It's enough.
No es bastante	It's not enough.
Es suyo.	It's yours.
Es mío.	It's mine.
Es nuestro.	It's ours.
Es para usted.	It's for you.
Es tarde.	It's late.
Es temprano.	It's early.
Está . . .	It is . . .
Está bien.	It's all right.
No está bien.	It's not all right.
Está mal.	It's bad.
Está muy mal.	It's very bad.
Está cerca.	It's near.
Está lejos.	It's far.
Está aquí.	It's here.
Está ahí.	It's there.
Está de moda.	It's chic. It's in style.

QUIZ 8

1.	*Es mucho.*	a.	It's enough.
2.	*Es fácil.*	b.	That isn't true.
3.	*Está cerca.*	c.	It's bad.
4.	*Es bastante.*	d.	It's near.
5.	*Eso no es verdad.*	e.	It's mine.

6. *Está mal.*	f. It's true.
7. *Es pequeño.*	g. It's here.
8. *Es verdad.*	h. It's small.
9. *Es mío.*	i. It's easy.
10. *Está aquí.*	j. It's a lot.

ANSWERS

1—j; 2—i; 3—d; 4—a; 5—b; 6—c; 7—h; 8—f; 9—e; 10—g.

C. To Have and Have Not: *TENER*

1. I HAVE

yo tengo	I have
tú tienes	you have
él tiene	he has
nosotros tenemos	we have
vosotros tenéis	you have
ellos tienen	they have

2. I DON'T HAVE

yo no tengo	I don't have
tú no tienes	you don't have
él no tiene	he doesn't have
nosotros no tenemos	we don't have
vosotros no tenéis	you don't have
ellos no tienen	they don't have

3. Study these phrases:

Tengo tiempo.	I have time.
No tengo tiempo.	I do not have any time.
No tiene dinero.	He does not have any money.
¿Tiene usted un cigarrillo?	Do you have a cigarette?

Tengo hambre.	I'm hungry. ("I have hunger.")
Tengo sed.	I'm thirsty. ("I have thirst.")
Tengo frío.	I'm cold. ("I have cold.")
Tengo calor.	I'm warm. ("I have warmth.")
Tengo razón.	I'm right. ("I have reason.")

See Lessons 27, 34, and 36 for more uses of *tener*.

D. WORD STUDY

comedia	comedy
constante	constant
contrario	contrary
deseo	desire
largo	long
del norte	north
órgano	organ
simple	simple
vendedor	vendor

LESSON 12

A. I ONLY KNOW A LITTLE SPANISH

¿Habla usted español?	Do you speak Spanish?
Sí, un poco.	Yes, a little.
Muy poco.	Very little.
No muy bien.	Not very well.
Hablo español.	I speak Spanish.
Lo hablo mal.	I speak it poorly.
No lo hablo muy bien.	I don't speak it very well.

Sólo sé unas cuantas palabras.	I only know a few words.
Sé decir algunas palabras en español.	I can say ("I know how to say") a few words in Spanish.
¿Habla su amigo español?	Does your friend speak Spanish?
No, mi amigo no habla español.	No, my friend doesn't speak Spanish.
¿Entiende usted el español?	Do you understand Spanish?
Sí, entiendo español.	Yes, I understand Spanish.
Lo entiendo pero no lo hablo.	I understand it but I don't speak it.
Lo leo pero no lo hablo.	I read it but I don't speak it.
No, no entiendo español.	No, I don't understand Spanish.
No entiendo muy bien el español.	I don't understand Spanish very well.
No lo pronuncio muy bien.	I don't pronounce it very well.
Me falta práctica.	I need practice. ("There is lacking to me practice.")
¿Me entiende?	Do you understand me?
Lo entiendo.[1]	I understand you.
No lo entiendo muy bien.[1]	I don't understand you very well.

[1] In Spain, you may also hear *le* meaning "you" in this context: *Le entiendo.* "I understand you." However, the forms above are correct and used more often in Latin America. Keep in mind that *Lo entiendo* can also mean "I understand it" (as seen above); the sentence context will clarify meaning.

¿Qué ha dicho usted?	What did you say?
¿Qué dijo usted?	What did you say?
Usted habla muy de prisa.	You speak too fast. You're speaking too fast.
No hable tan de prisa.	Don't speak so fast.
Hable más despacio.	Speak more slowly.
Tenga la bondad de hablar más despacio.	Please speak a little more slowly. ("Have the goodness to . . .")
Repita, por favor.	Please repeat.
Repítamelo.	Please repeat it ("to me").
¿Me entiende ahora?	Do you understand me now?
Ah, ya entiendo.	Oh, now I understand.
¿Qué quiere decir eso?	What does that mean?
¿Cómo se dice "Thanks" en español?	How do you say "Thanks" in Spanish?
¿Cómo se escribe esa palabra?	How do you spell ("write") that word?
Escríbamela, por favor.	Please write it down for me.

B. Do You Speak Spanish?

Buenos días, señor.	Good morning, sir.
Buenos días.	Good morning.

¿Habla usted español?	Do you speak Spanish?
Sí, hablo español.	Yes, I speak Spanish.
No hablo inglés.	I don't speak English.
¿Es usted sudamericano, señor?	Are you from South America?
Sí, soy chileno.	Yes, I'm from Chile. ("I'm a Chilean.")
¿Cuánto tiempo lleva usted en los Estados Unidos?	How long have you been in the United States?
Tres meses.	Three months.
Aprenderá inglés en poco tiempo. No es muy difícil.	You'll soon learn English. ("You'll learn English in little time.") It's not very hard.
Es más difícil de lo que usted piensa.	It's harder than you think.
Quizás tenga usted razón. Para nosotros es más fácil aprender español[1] que para ustedes inglés.[1]	You're probably right. Spanish is easier for us to learn than English is for you. ("For us it is easier to learn Spanish than for you English.")
Usted habla muy bien el español.	You speak Spanish very well.
Viví en México por varios años.	I lived in Mexico for several years.
Tiene usted una pronunciación muy buena.	You have an excellent pronunciation.

[1] *El español* and *el inglés* are also correct to use.

Muchas gracias. Sin embargo, necesito practicar.	Thank you. I need practice though. ("Nevertheless, I need to practice.")
Tendré que marcharme. Va a salir mi tren.	I'll have to leave now. My train's about to leave. ("My train's going to go.")
Buena suerte y buen viaje.	Good luck and a pleasant trip.
Lo mismo le deseo a usted.	The same to you. ("I wish you the same.")
Adiós.	Good-bye.

QUIZ 9

1. *Lo entiendo pero no lo hablo.*
2. *¿Me entiende ahora?*
3. *No lo hablo muy bien.*
4. *Usted habla muy de prisa.*
5. *¿Cómo se escribe esa palabra?*
6. *¿Habla usted español?*
7. *Necesito practicar.*

a. Do you speak Spanish?
b. I need to practice.
c. a little
d. What did you say?
e. Repeat it to me.
f. We have money.
g. I'm thirsty.

8. *un poco*	h. I understand it but I don't speak it.
9. *Repítamelo.*	i. Speak more slowly.
10. *Tenemos dinero.*	j. I don't speak it very well.
11. *Hable más despacio.*	k. How do you say "Thanks" in Spanish?
12. *Lo hablo mal.*	l. You speak too fast.
13. *¿Qué ha dicho usted?*	m. Do you understand me now?
14. *¿Cómo se dice "Thanks" en español?*	n. How do you spell that word?
15. *Tengo sed.*	o. I speak it poorly.

ANSWERS
1—h; 2—m; 3—j; 4—l; 5—n; 6—a; 7—b; 8—c;
9—e; 10—f; 11—i; 12—o; 13—d; 14—k; 15—g.

C. EXCUSE ME AND THANK YOU

Perdón.	Pardon me. Excuse me.
Perdone usted.	I beg your pardon.
Dispense usted.	Excuse me.
¿Me hace el favor de repetirlo?	Please repeat. ("Will you do me the favor of repeating it?")
Con gusto.	With pleasure. Gladly.
Con mucho gusto.	With great pleasure. Very gladly.
Con muchísimo gusto.	With the greatest pleasure.

Estoy a sus órdenes.	I'm at your disposal ("orders").
¿En qué puedo servirle?	What can I do for you? ("In what can I serve you?")
Usted es muy amable.	You're very kind. That's very kind of you.
Usted es muy atento.	You're very kind. That's very kind of you.
Gracias.	Thanks.
Muchas gracias.	Many thanks.
Muchísimas gracias.	Thanks a lot. ("Very many thanks.")
Un millón de gracias.	Thanks very much. ("A million thanks.")
De nada.	You're welcome.
No hay de qué.	You're welcome.
No es nada.	It's nothing.

D. WORD STUDY

cadena	chain
carta	letter
completo	complete
crema	cream
eterno	eternal
fuente	fountain
oficial	officer
sistema	system

LESSON 13

A. THIS AND THAT (DEMONSTRATIVE PRONOUNS AND ADJECTIVES)

1. Demonstrative pronouns:

Deme éste.	Give me this one *(masc.)*.
Deme ésta.	Give me this one *(fem.)*.
Deme éstos.	Give me these *(masc.)*.
Deme éstas.	Give me these *(fem.)*.
Deme ése.	Give me that one *(masc.)*.
Deme ésa.	Give me that one *(fem.)*.
Deme ésos.	Give me those *(masc.)*.
Deme ésas.	Give me those *(fem.)*.
Deme aquél.	Give me that one over there *(refers to something farther away)*.
Deme aquélla.	Give me that one *(fem.)* over there.
Deme aquéllos.	Give me those over there.
Deme aquéllas.	Give me those *(fem.)* over there.

Note the following neuter forms for this and that. They refer to an idea, statement, or anything not specifically mentioned:

Deme esto.	Give me this.
Deme eso.	Give me that.
Deme aquello.	Give me that one over there.

2. Demonstrative adjectives:
These forms without the written accent mark also come before nouns as demonstrative adjectives:

este muchacho	this boy
esta señora	this lady
esa señora	that lady
aquel señor	that gentleman over there
aquellos vecinos	those neighbors over there

QUIZ 10

1. *Deme éstos.*	a.	Give me those over there.
2. *Éste.*	b.	That one over there.
3. *Deme ésa.*	c.	This lady.
4. *Este muchacho.*	d.	This one.
5. *Ése.*	e.	That gentleman over there.
6. *Aquellos vecinos.*	f.	This boy.
7. *Deme aquéllos.*	g.	Give me these.
8. *Aquél.*	h.	That one.
9. *Esta señora.*	i.	Those neighbors over there.
10. *Aquel señor.*	j.	Give me that one *(fem.).*

ANSWERS
1—g; 2—d; 3—j; 4—f; 5—h; 6—i; 7—a; 8—b; 9 c; 10 e.

B. MORE OR LESS

1. More

más despacio	more slowly
más difícil	more difficult
más fácil	easier
más lejos	farther
más cerca	nearer
más que eso	more than that
más de un año	more than a year

2. Less

menos despacio	less slowly
menos difícil	less difficult
menos fácil	less easy
menos lejos	less far, not so far
menos cerca	less near, not so near
menos que eso	less than that
menos de un año	less than a year

C. AND, OR, BUT

1. *y* "and"

Roberto y Juan son hermanos.	Robert and John are brothers.

> *e* is used instead of *y* before words beginning with *i-* or *hi-:*

María e Isabel son hermanas.	Mary and Elizabeth are sisters
Madre e hija.	Mother and daughter.

2. *o* "or"

Cinco o seis pesos.	Five or six pesos.
Voy con mi hermano o con mi hermana.	I'm going with my brother or (with) my sister.

> *u* is used instead of *o* before words beginning with *o* or *ho*.

siete u ocho horas	seven or eight hours
cinco u ocho meses	five or eight months
mujeres u hombres	women or men

3. *pero* "but"

Quiero ir pero no sé cuando.	I want to go but I don't know when.
Quiero ir pero no puedo.	I want to go but I can't.
Yo voy pero ella no va.	I'm going but she isn't going.

4. *sino* "but" is used instead of *pero* after a negative statement:

No es francés sino inglés.	He is not French but English.
No viene hoy sino mañana.	He is not coming today but tomorrow.

D. WORD STUDY

banda	band
chofer	chauffeur
composición	composition
conciencia	conscience
decoración	decoration
misión	mission
numeral	numeral
ordinario	common
región	region

QUIZ 11

1. *inglés*
2. *y*
3. *pero*

a. five or six days
b. He is not French but English.
c. seven or eight hours

4. *hija*	d. English
5. *hermano*	e. but
6. *cinco o seis días*	f. tomorrow
7. *cuando*	g. daughter
8. *No es francés sino inglés.*	h. and
9. *mañana*	i. when
10. *siete u ocho horas*	j. brother

ANSWERS

1—d; 2—h; 3—e; 4—g; 5—j; 6—a; 7—i; 8—b; 9—f;
10—c.

REVIEW QUIZ 2

1. _____ (This) *muchacho.*
   a. *esta*
   b. *este*
   c. *esa*

2. *Deme* _____ (those *fem.*).
   a. *ésas*
   b. *éstos*
   c. *aquél*

3. *El gusto es* _____ (mine).
   a. *yo*
   b. *mío*
   c. *mucho*

4. *¿Cómo* _____ (are) *usted?*
   a. *estás*
   b. *tiene*
   c. *está*

5. _____ (It's) *necesario*.
   a. *Es*
   b. *Está*
   c. *Tiene*

6. _____ (We are) *de España*.
   a. *Están*
   b. *Somos*
   c. *Son*

7. _____ (More) *difícil*.
   a. *Más*
   b. *Menos*
   c. *Cuándo*

8. *Roberto y Juan* _____ (have) *mucho dinero*.
   a. *tengo*
   b. *tienen*
   c. *tenemos*

9. *Cinco* _____ (or) *seis pesos*.
   a. *o*
   b. *sino*
   c. *y*

10. *Quiero venir* _____ (but) *no puedo*.
    a. *o*
    b. *pero*
    c. *sino*

ANSWERS
1—b; 2—a; 3—b; 4—c; 5—a; 6—b; 7—a; 8—b;
9—a; 10—b.

LESSON 14

A. WHERE?

¿Dónde?	Where?
¿Dónde está?	Where is (it)?
Aquí.	Here.
Allí.	There.
A la derecha.	To the right.
A la izquierda.	To the left.
Está en la calle de Alcalá.	It's on Alcala Street.
Está en la plaza de Santa Ana.	It's on Santa Ana Square.
Está en la avenida de Mayo.	It's on Mayo Avenue.
¿Por dónde?	Which way?
Por aquí.	This way.
Por allí.	That way.
¿Cómo se va allí?	How do you get there?
¿Dónde es eso?	Where's the place you're talking about? ("Where is that?")
Es aquí.	It's here.
Es allí.	It's there.
¿Dónde está el libro?	Where's the book?
Está aquí.	It's here.
¿Dónde está usted?	Where are you?
Aquí estoy.	Here I am.
¿Dónde están ustedes?	Where are you?
Aquí estamos.	Here we are.

B. HERE AND THERE

Está aquí.	It's here.
Aquí está.	Here it is.

Está aquí mismo.	It's right here.
Está ahí.	It's there *(where you are)*.
Está allí.	It's over there *(distant from both of us)*.
Aquí está.	Here he is.
Está aquí.	He's here.
Está ahí.	He's there.
Ahí va.	There he goes.
Está por ahí.	He's somewhere over there.
Póngalo aquí.	Put it here.
Póngalo ahí.	Put it there.
Espéreme aquí.	Wait for me here.
Espéreme ahí.	Wait for me there.
Venga usted acá.	Come here.
Acá viene.	Here he comes.
Vaya usted allá.	Go there.
Allá lejos.	Way over there.
Aquí cerca.	Around here. Near here.
Allá en España.	Over there in Spain.
Aquí en América.	Here in America.
Allá dentro.	In there.
Allá fuera.	Out there.
¿Dónde vive?	Where does he live?
Vive allí.	He lives there.
Espero verlo allí.	I expect to see him there.
Ella está allí.	She's there.
¿Es aquí donde vive Juan?	Does John live here? Is this where John lives?
Aquí es.	This is the place. It's here.

No es aquí.	It's not here.
Es allí.	It's there.
Vaya usted por aquí.	Go this way.
Vaya usted por allí.	Go that way.
Entre usted por aquí.	Come in this way.
Salga por allí.	Go out that way.

NOTE:

a. *Aquí* "here" refers to something near the speaker:

Tengo aquí los libros.	I have the books here.

b. *Ahí* "there" refers to something near the person spoken to:

c. *Allí* "there" refers to something remote from both:

Vienen de allí.	They've come from there.
Viví en Sur América por varios años. ¿Ha estado usted allí?	I lived in South America for several years. Have you ever been there?
¿Qué tiene usted ahí?	What do you have there?
¿Está usted ahí?	Are you there?

d. *Acá* "here" expresses motion toward the speaker:

¡Venga usted acá!	Come here!

e. *Allá* "there" indicates motion away from the speaker:

Vaya usted allá.	Go there.
Mañana voy allá.	Tomorrow I'm going there.

f. *Por aquí* means "this way" or "around here"; *por allí* means "that way" or "around there":

Vaya usted por aquí.	Go this way.

C. To the Right, etc.

A la derecha.	To the right.
A la izquierda.	To the left.
En la esquina.	On the corner.
Todo derecho.	Straight ahead.
Vaya usted todo derecho.	Go straight ahead.
Doble usted a la derecha.	Turn (to your) right.
Doble a la izquierda.	Turn (to your) left.

D. Near and Far

Está cerca.	It's near. It's nearby.
Cerca de aquí.	Near here.
Muy cerca.	Very near.
A dos pasos de aquí.	A few steps from here.
Cerca del pueblo.	Near the town.
Cerca del parque.	Near the park.
Al lado de la iglesia.	Next to the church.
¿Está cerca de aquí?	Is it near here?
¿Está lejos?	Is it far?
¿Está lejos de aquí?	Is it far from here?
Está muy lejos.	It's very far.
No está tan lejos.	It's not too far.
No está muy lejos.	It's not too far.

Es más adelante.	It's farther.
Es un poco más allá.	It's a little farther.
¿Cuánto hay de aquí a allí?	How far is it from here to there?
Está a dos cuadras de aquí.	It's two blocks from here.
Está a una milla de aquí.	It's a ("one") mile from here.

QUIZ 12

1. *¿Dónde está?*   a. I expect to see him there.
2. *Espéreme aquí.*   b. Which way?
3. *Aquí.*   c. To the left.
4. *A la derecha.*   d. It's far.
5. *Allí.*   e. Here.
6. *Es aquí mismo.*   f. Wait for me here.
7. *Espero verlo allí.*   g. Straight ahead.
8. *A la izquierda.*   h. To the right.
9. *Está lejos.*   i. There.
10. *¿Por dónde?*   j. Out there.
11. *Está por ahí.*   k. Go that way.
12. *Está cerca.*   l. It's right here.
13. *Allá fuera.*   m. Where is it?
14. *Vaya usted por allí.*   n. He's somewhere around here.
15. *Todo derecho.*   o. It's near.

ANSWERS

1—m; 2—f; 3—e; 4—h; 5—i; 6—l; 7—a; 8—c; 9—d; 10—b; 11—n; 12—o; 13—j; 14—k; 15—g.

LESSON 15

A. I, You, He, etc. (Subject Pronouns)

SINGULAR

yo	I
tú	you *(fam.)*
él	he
ella	she
ello	it
usted	you *(pol.)*

(yo) hablo	I speak
(tú) hablas	you speak *(fam.)*
(él) habla	he speaks
(ella) habla	she speaks
(usted) habla	you speak

PLURAL

nosotros	we *(masc.)*
nosotras	we *(fem.)*
vosotros	you *(masc.)*
vosotras	you *(fem.)*
ellos	they *(masc.)*
ellas	they *(fem.)*
ustedes	you *(pol.)*

(nosotros) hablamos	we speak
(nosotras) hablamos	we speak *(fem.)*
(vosotros) habláis	you speak
(vosotras) habláis	you speak *(fem.)*
(ellos) hablan	they speak
(ellas) hablan	they speak *(fem.)*
(ustedes) hablan	you speak

The personal pronouns *yo, tú*, etc., are not ordinarily used; "I speak" is just *hablo,* "we speak" *hablamos,* etc. They are used only for emphasis or clearness.

B. It's Me (I), You, He, etc.

Soy yo.	It's me (I).
Eres tú.	It's you.
Es usted.	It's you *(pol.)*.
Es él.	It's he.
Es ella.	It's she.

Somos nosotros.	It's us (we).
Sois vosotros.	It's you *(masc.)*.
Sois vosotras.	It's you *(fem.)*.
Son ellos.	It's them (they) *(masc.)*.
Son ellas.	It's them (they) *(fem.)*.
Son ustedes.	It's you *(pol.)*.

C. It and Them (Direct Object Pronouns[1])

	SINGULAR	PLURAL
MASCULINE	*lo* it	*los* them
FEMININE	*la* it	*las* them

¿Tiene usted el dinero?	Do you have the money?
Sí, lo tengo.	Yes, I have it.
¿Tiene usted la carta?	Do you have the letter?
Sí, la tengo.	Yes, I have it.
¿Vio usted a Juan y a Pedro?	Did you see John and Peter?
Sí, los vi.	Yes, I saw them.

[1] See Lesson 16 item D for more on object pronouns.

¿Vio usted a María y a Carmen?	Did you see Mary and Carmen?
Sí, las vi.	Yes, I saw them.

N O T E :

a. The pronoun is masculine if the word it refers to is masculine, plural if the word it refers to is plural, etc.

b. *Lo* is used for "it" when the reference is to an idea or a whole expression:

Lo comprendo.	I understand it.

c. These forms usually come immediately before the conjugated verb. In case of the infinitive ("to understand," etc.) they could also follow:

Quiere comprenderlo.	He wants to understand it.

LESSON 16

A. My, Your, His, etc. (Possessive Adjectives)

There are two forms for the adjectives *"my," "your," "his,"* etc.—one that precedes the noun (the more common one) and one that follows (more emphatic):

1. Preceding the Noun

mi (pl. *mis*)	my
tu (pl. *tus*)	your *(fam.)*
su (pl. *sus*)	his, her, your *(pol.)*

nuestro, -a (pl. *-os, -as*)	our
vuestro, -a (pl. *-os, -as*)	your *(fam.)*
su (pl. *sus*)	their, your *(pol.)*

NOTE:

a. To clarify the meaning of *su, sus* in a sentence, the definite article may be used in their place along with *de Ud., de él, de Uds., de ellos, de ellas:*

| *sus vestidos* | his, her, your, their dresses |
| *los vestidos de ellas* | their *(fem.)* dresses |

b. Use the definite article in place of the possessive adjective for body parts, and clothing that is obviously owned by the subject:

| *Marcos se pone el sombrero.* | Mark puts his hat on. |
| *Me lavo la cara.* | I wash my face. |

2. Following the Noun

The forms of the possessive adjectives below must be preceded by *el, la, los,* or *las* (except when you are talking to someone directly).

mío, mía (pl. *-os, -as*)	(of) mine
tuyo, -a (pl. *-os, -as*)	(of) yours
suyo, -a (pl. *-os, -as*)	(of) his, her, your
nuestro, -a (pl. *-os, -as*)	(of) ours
vuestro, -a (pl. *-os, -as*)	(of) yours *(fam.)*
suyo, -a (pl. *-os, -as*)	(of) yours, theirs
el sombrero mío	my hat
la casa tuya	your *(fam.)* house

When *un, una, unos, unas* are used with these forms of possessive adjectives, they mean "of mine, of yours, of his," etc.

un amigo mío   a friend of mine

3. Study the following examples:

SINGULAR

mi amigo	my friend
tu amigo	your friend
su amigo	his, her, your friend
nuestro amigo	our friend
nuestra amiga	our friend
vuestro amigo	your friend
vuestra amiga	your friend
su amigo	their friend, your friend

PLURAL

mis amigos	my friends
tus amigos	your friends
sus amigos	his, her, your friends
nuestros amigos	our friends
nuestras amigas	our friends
vuestros amigos	your friends
vuestras amigas	your friends
sus amigos	their friends, your friends

SINGULAR

mi sombrero	my hat
tu vestido	your dress
su vestido	her dress, their dress
nuestro amigo	our friend
nuestra madre	our mother
vuestro hijo	your son
vuestra hija	your daughter

PLURAL

mis sombreros	my hats
tus vestidos	your dresses
sus vestidos	her dresses, their dresses
nuestros amigos	our friends
nuestras madres	our mothers
vuestros hijos	your sons
vuestras hijas	your daughters

4. Other Examples:

MASCULINE SINGULAR

¿Dónde está mi hermano?	Where is my brother?
¿Dónde está tu hermano?	Where is your brother?
¿Dónde está su hermano?	Where is his (her, your) brother?
¿Dónde está nuestro hermano?	Where is our brother?
¿Dónde está vuestro hermano?	Where is your brother?
¿Dónde está su hermano?	Where is their (your) brother?

FEMININE SINGULAR

¿Dónde está mi hermana?	Where is my sister?
¿Dónde está tu hermana?	Where is your sister?
¿Dónde está su hermana?	Where is his (her, your) sister?
¿Dónde está nuestra hermana?	Where is our sister?
¿Dónde está vuestra hermana?	Where is your sister?

¿Dónde está su *hermana?*	Where is their (your) sister?

MASCULINE PLURAL

¿Dónde están mis *libros?*	Where are my books?
¿Dónde están tus *libros?*	Where are your books?
¿Dónde están sus *libros?*	Where are his (her, your) books?
¿Dónde están nuestros *libros?*	Where are our books?
¿Dónde están vuestros libros?	Where are your books?
¿Dónde están sus libros?	Where are their (your) books?

FEMININE PLURAL

¿Dónde están mis cartas?	Where are my letters?
¿Dónde están tus cartas?	Where are your letters?
¿Dónde están sus *cartas?*	Where are his (her, your) letters
¿Dónde están nuestras *cartas?*	Where are our letters?
¿Dónde están vuestras *cartas?*	Where are your letters?
¿Dónde están sus *cartas?*	Where are their (your) letters?

B. ITS, MINE, YOURS, HIS, ETC. (POSSESSIVE PRONOUNS)

The possessive pronouns are used with the articles *el, la, los, las.* The articles are omitted after the verb *ser.*

1. With the definite article

Tiene el mío, *la mía; los míos, las mías*	He has mine.
Tiene el tuyo, *la tuya; etc.*	He has yours.
Tiene el suyo, *la suya; etc.*	He has his (hers, yours).
Tiene el nuestro, *la nuestra; etc.*	He has ours.
Tiene el vuestro, *la vuestra; etc.*	He has yours.
Tiene el suyo, *la suya; etc.*	He has theirs (yours).

2. Without definite articles

Es mío, *-a; Son míos, -as*	It's mine. They're mine.
Es tuyo, *-a; Son tuyos, -as*	It's yours. They're yours.
Es suyo, *-a; Son suyos, -as*	It's his (hers, yours). They're his (hers, yours).
Es nuestro, *-a; Son nuestros, -as*	It's ours. They're ours.
Es vuestro, *-a; Son vuestros, -as*	It's yours. They're yours.
Es suyo, -a; Son suyos, -as	It's theirs. They're theirs (yours).

NOTE:

a. When the pronoun is plural, *son* is used instead of *es*, and *los/las* instead of *el/la*.

b. For clarity, *el suyo, la suya, los suyos, las suyas* are replaced often by *el de Ud., el de él, el de ella,*

el de Uds., el de ellos, el de ellas:
La de ella es grande. Hers is big.

3. Other examples:

Mis amigos y los tuyos.	My friends and yours.
Su libro es mejor que el nuestro.	His book is better than ours.
¿De quién es la carta?—Es suya.	Whose letter is this?— It's his.

C. PREPOSITIONAL PRONOUNS

Some pronouns have a different form when they come after a preposition:

para mí	for me
por ti	for your sake
con él	with him
a ella	to her
para usted	for you
sin nosotros	without us
con vosotros[1]	with you
para ellos	for them (*masc.*)
para ellas	for them (*fem.*)
de ustedes	of, about you
Hablo de ti.	I'm speaking about you.
Juan va sin nosotros.	John is going without us.

---

[1] Irregular forms of the prepositional pronouns occur with *con: conmigo* = with me; *contigo* = with you; *consigo* = with yourself/himself/herself/themselves.

Quiere ir conmigo.   He wants to go with
                                me.

Habla de él.   He (she) is speaking
                                about him.

D. DIRECT AND INDIRECT OBJECT PRONOUNS

1. Direct object pronouns take the place of the
   direct object in a sentence; they directly receive
   the action of the verb. On page 72 the terms *lo/la*
   (him/her and it) and *los/las* (them, *masc.* and
   fem.) appeared. The following group of phrases
   shows all the direct object pronouns:

   a. He understands me.

Juan me entiende.   John understands me.
Juan te entiende.   John understands you
                                (fam.).
Juan lo entiende.   John understands him/
                                it/you *(pol. masc.).*
Juan la entiende.   John understands her/it/
                                you *(pol. fem.).*
Juan nos entiende.   John understands us.
Juan os entiende.   John understands you
                                (fam. pl.).
Juan los entiende.   John understands them/
                                you *(pol. pl. masc.).*
Juan las entiende.   John understands them/
                                you *(pol. pl. fem.).*

b. She buys it

Anna la compra.	Anna buys it *(a fem. noun).*
Anna lo compra.	Anna buys it *(a masc. noun).*
Anna las compra.	Anna buys them *(fem. nouns).*
Anna los compra.	Anna buys them (masc. nouns).

c. Glad to see you!

Mucho gusto en (de) verlo!	Glad to see you (a man)!
Mucho gusto en (de) verla!	Glad to see you (a woman)!
Mucho gusto en (de) verlos!	Glad to see you (several men or a group of men and women)!
Mucho gusto en (de) verlas!	Glad to see you (several women)!

Notice the use of *lo, la, los, las* in the *usted* form—that is, the form you use in speaking to people whom you don't know very well or with whom your relationship is rather formal.

2. Indirect object pronouns indicate the person to, for, or from whom any action occurs. (In English, you sometimes use "to" before the indirect object pronoun.) The forms of these pronouns are the same as the direct object pronouns, except for the third-person singular and plural (*le* and *les*):

a. He told me

Me dijo.	He (she) told me.
Te dijo.	He (she) told you *(fam.)*.
Le dijo.	He (she) told you *(pol.)*/him/her.
Nos dijo.	He (she) told us.
Os dijo.	He (she) told you *(fam. pl.)*.
Les dijo.	He (she) told you *(pol. pl.)*/them.

b. I'm speaking to you

Te hablo.	I'm speaking to you *(fam.)*.
Le hablo.	I'm speaking to you *(pol.)*/him/her.
Me habla.	He (she) is speaking to me.
Les hablo.	I'm speaking to you *(pol. pl.)*/them.
Nos hablan.	They are speaking to us.

c. The pronoun is always repeated for clarity or emphasis:

¿Qué le pasa a usted?	What's the matter with you?
Le doy el libro.	I give him/her/you the book.
Le doy el libro a él.	I give the book to him.
Le doy el libro a ella.	I give the book to her.
Le doy el libro a usted.	I give the book to you.
A mí me gusta el libro.	I like the book.

3. When there are two object pronouns in a sentence, the indirect precedes the direct, and both precede the conjugated verb[1]:

---

[1] See the Summary of Spanish Grammar, Position of Pronouns.

Me lo dijo.	He (she) told it to me.
Te lo dijo.	He (she) told it to you *(fam.)*.
Se lo dijo.	He (she) told it to you *(pol.)*.
Se lo dijo.	He (she) told it to him/her.
Nos lo dijo.	He (she) told it to us.
Os lo dijo.	He (she) told it to you *(fam.)*.
Se lo dijo.	He (she) told it to you *(pol.)*.
Se lo dijo.	He (she) told it to them.

NOTE:

a. *Se* replaces *le* or *les* (the indirect object) before *lo, la, los, las* (direct objects):

Juan le da el libro.	John gives the book to him/her.
Juan se lo da.	John gives it to him/her.

b. Since *se* has several meanings, to clarify add *a él, a ella, a Ud., a ellos, a ellas, a Uds.:*

Juan se lo da a ella.	John gives it to her.

4. The preposition *a* ("personal *a*") is used before the direct object of a verb if the direct object is a definite person, persons, or pronoun referring to a person; in some countries with a pet; and most geographic names. It is not used with the verb *tener.*

Veo a mis amigos.	I see my friends.
Veo a Marcos.	I see Mark.
No veo a nadie.	I see no one.
Busca a su gato.	He looks for his cat.
Visito a Chile.	I visit Chile.

| **Tiene un hermano.** | He has a brother. |
| **Invita a dos amigas.** | He invites two friends. |

E. MYSELF, YOURSELF, HIMSELF, ETC. (REFLEXIVE PRONOUNS)

Yo me lavo.	I wash myself.
Tú te lavas.	You wash yourself.
El se lava.	He washes himself.
Ella se lava.	She washes herself.
Usted se lava.	You wash yourself.
Nosotros nos lavamos.	We wash ourselves.
Vosotros os laváis.	You wash yourselves.
Ellos se lavan.	They wash themselves.

Other Examples:

| **¿Cómo se llama usted?** | What's your name? ("What do you call yourself?") |
| **Nos vemos en el espejo.** | We see ourselves in the mirror. |

1. Notice the forms for "myself," "yourself," etc.: *me, te, se,* etc. Verbs which take these "reflexive pronouns" are called "reflexive" verbs. Many verbs are reflexive in Spanish which are not in English:

| **Me divierto.** | I'm having a good time. |

Me engaño.	I'm mistaken.
Me siento.	I sit down. I'm sitting down.
Me levanto.	I get up. I'm getting up (standing up).
Me voy.	I'm going away. I'm leaving.
Se me ocurre.	I have an idea. It occurs to me.
Se me olvida.	I forget.
Se me figura.	I imagine.

2. In Spanish you don't say "I'm washing my hands" but "I'm washing the hands"; not "Take your hat off" but "Take off the hat":

Me lavo las manos.	I'm washing my hands.
Quítese el sombrero.	Take your hat off.
Se ha roto el brazo.	He broke (has broken) his arm.
Me duele la cabeza.	I have a headache.
Me duele el estómago.	I have a stomachache.
Se ha cortado un dedo.	She's cut her finger.
Me he lastimado la mano.	I've hurt my hand.

3. *Se* can also be used as a subject. It is called the impersonal *se* and it implies the meaning of "someone." It is often used where we would use the passive in English.

Aquí se habla español.	Spanish spoken here.
Se abren las puertas a las ocho.	The doors are opened at eight.

4. The reflexive forms are also often used to translate our "one," "they," "people," etc.

Se dice que . . .	It's said that . . . People say that . . . They say that . . .
Se come bien aquí.	The food's good here. ("One eats well here.")

F. WORD STUDY

desarrollo	development
diversión	diversion
líquido	liquid
obligación	obligation
ocupación	occupation
pálido	pale
popular	popular
sólido	solid
teatro	theater
viaje	voyage

QUIZ 13

1. *Me siento.*	a. I get up.
2. *Se me ocurre.*	b. I'm leaving.
3. *Me divierto.*	c. I forget.
4. *Se me figura.*	d. I'm mistaken.
5. *Me levanto.*	e. I wash myself.
6. *Me lavo.*	f. I'm having a good time.

7. *Me engaño.*	g. They bathe them-selves.
8. *Se bañen.*	h. I imagine.
9. *Se me olvida.*	i. It occurs to me.
10. *Me voy.*	j. I sit down.

ANSWERS
1—j; 2—i;3—f; 4—h; 5—a; 6—e; 7—d; 8—g; 9—c;
10—b.

REVIEW QUIZ 3

1. *Es* _____ (she).
    a. *él*
    b. *ella*
    c. *yo*

2. *Somos* _____ (us).
    a. *ellos*
    b. *tú*
    c. *nosotros*

3. *Le doy el libro a* _____ (him).
    a. *él*
    b. *usted*
    c. *lo*

4. *Es* _____ (her) *vestido*.
    a. *su*
    b. *mi*
    c. *nuestro*

5. *Son* _____ (our) *cartas*.
    a. *nuestro*
    b. *nuestras*
    c. *tuyo*

6. *¿Dónde están* _____ (my) *libros?*
   a. *tus*
   b. *mis*
   c. *nuestra*

7. *Su libro es mejor que el* _____ (ours).
   a. *tuyos*
   b. *nuestro*
   c. *su*

8. *Hablamos de* _____ (you).
   a. *ti*
   b. *ellos*
   c. *él*

9. _____ (To us) *lo dio.*
   a. *Se*
   b. *Nos*
   c. *Nosotros*

10. *¿Cómo se* _____ (call) *usted?*
    a. *lavo*
    b. *llama*
    c. *vemos*

11. *Quiere ir* _____ (with me).
    a. *consigo*
    b. *sin mí*
    c. *conmigo*

12. *Me* _____ (mistaken).
    a. *engaño*
    b. *levanto*
    c. *ocurre*

13. *Te* _____ (sit down).
    a. *voy*
    b. *figure*
    c. *sientas*

14. *Nos* _____ (wash) *las manos*.
    a. *roto*
    b. *lavamos*
    c. *lastimado*

15. *Me* _____ (leaving, going away).
    a. *voy*
    b. *vemos*
    c. *llama*

ANSWERS
1—b; 2—c;3—a; 4—a; 5—b; 6—b; 7—b; 8—a;
9—b; 10—b; 11—c; 12—a; 13—c; 14—b; 15—a.

LESSON 17

A. SOME ACTION PHRASES

¡Voy!	I'm coming!
¡Ya voy!	I'm coming right away!
En seguida.	Immediately.
Voy en seguida.	I'm coming immediately.
¡Vámonos!	Let's go!
¡Venga en seguida!	Come quickly!
¡Dese prisa!	Hurry up!
¡Apúrese!	Hurry up!
No se de prisa.	Don't rush.
No se apure.	Don't rush.

Tengo prisa.	I'm in a hurry.
No tengo prisa.	I'm not in a hurry.
¡Rápido!	Quickly!
Más despacio.	Slower.
Ahora mismo.	Right now.
¡Un momento!	One moment! Just a minute!
Pronto.	Soon.
Inmediatamente.	Immediately.
Más pronto.	Sooner.
Más tarde.	Later.
De repente.	Suddenly.
¡Cuidado!	Watch out!

QUIZ 14

1. *¡Cuidado!*   a. Slower.
2. *Tengo prisa.*   b. Right now.
3. *¡Un momento!*   c. Come right away.
4. *Pronto.*   d. I'm coming right away!
5. *Inmediatamente.*   e. Watch out!
6. *Más tarde.*   f. Later.
7. *Más despacio.*   g. I'm in a hurry.
8. *¡Ya voy!*   h. Just a minute!
9. *Venga en seguida.*   i. Immediately.
10. *Ahora mismo.*   j. Soon.

ANSWERS
1—e; 2—g;3—h; 4—j; 5—i; 6—f; 7—a; 8—d; 9—c; 10—b.

B. CAN YOU TELL ME?

¿Me permite que le haga una pregunta?	May I ask you a question?
¿Permítame que le pregunte . . . ?	May I ask (you) . . . ?
¿Puede decirme?	Can you tell me?
¿Podría decirme?	Could you tell me?
¿Quiere decirme?	Will you tell me?
Dígame, por favor.	Tell me, please.
Haga el favor de decirme.	Could you please tell me?
¿Qué quiere usted decir?	What do you mean?
Quiero decir que . . .	I mean that . . .
¿Qué quiere decir eso?	What docs that mcan?
Esto quiere decir . . .	This means . . .

C. WORD STUDY

barrera	barrier
carácter	character
curioso	curious
curiosidad	curiosity
diccionario	dictionary
grado	degree
militar	army
muchas veces	often
oficial	official
piedad	pity

LESSON 18

A. NUMBERS

1. One through One Thousand

uno	one
dos	two
tres	three
cuatro	four
cinco	five
seis	six
siete	seven
ocho	eight
nueve	nine
diez	ten
once	eleven
doce	twelve
trece	thirteen
catorce	fourteen
quince	fifteen
dieciséis *(diez y seis)*	sixteen
diecisiete *(diez y siete)*	seventeen
dieciocho *(diez y ocho)*	eighteen
diecinueve *(diez y nueve)*	nineteen
veinte	twenty
veintiuno *(veinte y uno)*	twenty-one
veintidós *(veinte y dos)*	twenty-two
veintitrés *(veinte y tres)*	twenty-three
treinta	thirty
treinta y uno	thirty-one
treinta y dos	thirty-two
treinta y tres	thirty-three
cuarenta	forty
cuarenta y uno	forty-one

cuarenta y dos	forty-two
cuarenta y tres	forty-three
cincuenta	fifty
cincuenta y uno	fifty-one
cincuenta y dos	fifty-two
cincuenta y tres	fifty-three
sesenta	sixty
sesenta y uno	sixty-one
sesenta y dos	sixty-two
sesenta y tres	sixty-three
setenta	seventy
setenta y uno	seventy-one
setenta y dos	seventy-two
setenta y tres	seventy-three
ochenta	eighty
ochenta y uno	eighty-one
ochenta y dos	eighty-two
ochenta y tres	eighty-three
noventa	ninety
noventa y uno	ninety-one
noventa y dos	ninety-two
noventa y tres	ninety-three
cien	hundred
ciento uno	a hundred and one
ciento dos	a hundred and two
ciento tres	a hundred and three
mil	thousand
mil uno	a thousand and one
mil dos	a thousand and two
mil tres	a thousand and three

B. MORE NUMBERS

1.
120	**ciento veinte**
122	**ciento veintidós (ciento veinte y dos)**
130	**ciento treinta**
140	**ciento cuarenta**
150	**ciento cincuenta**
160	**ciento sesenta**
170	**ciento setenta**
171	**ciento setenta y uno**
178	**ciento setenta y ocho**
180	**ciento ochenta**
182	**ciento ochenta y dos**
190	**ciento noventa**
198	**ciento noventa y ocho**
199	**ciento noventa y nueve**
200	**doscientos**
324	**trescientos veinte y cuatro**
555	**quinientos cincuenta y cinco**
875	**ochocientos setenta y cinco**
932	**novecientos treinta y dos**

2. First, Second, Third

primero, -a	first
segundo, -a	second
tercero, -a	third
cuarto, -a	fourth
quinto, -a	fifth
sexto, -a	sixth
séptimo, -a	seventh
octavo, -a	eighth
noveno, -a	ninth
décimo, -a	tenth

3. Two and Two

Dos y dos son cuatro.	Two and two are four.
Dos más dos son cuatro.	Two and two are four.
Cuatro más dos son seis.	Four and two are six.
Diez menos dos son ocho.	Ten minus two is eight.

QUIZ 15

1. *mil*	a. 1002
2. *once*	b. 32
3. *cien*	c. 102
4. *diecisiete*	d. 324
5. *treinta*	e. 11
6. *veinte*	f. 1000
7. *sesenta*	g. 60
8. *trescientos veinticuatro*	h. 71
9. *treinta y dos*	i. 17
10. *ciento dos*	j. 875
11. *ochocientos setenta y cinco*	k. 83
12. *setenta y uno*	l. 93
13. *mil dos*	m. 20
14. *noventa y tres*	n. 30
15. *ochenta y tres*	o. 100

ANSWERS
1—f; 2—e;3—o; 4—i; 5—n; 6—m; 7—g; 8—d;
9—b; 10—c; 11—j; 12—h; 13—a; 14—l; 15—k.

C. WORD STUDY

absoluto	absolute
aspecto	aspect
barra	bar
cambio	exchange
cierto	certain
combinación	combination
manera	manner
peligro	danger

LESSON 19

A. HOW MUCH?

¿Cuánto cuesta esto?	How much does this cost?
Cuesta cuarenta centavos.	It costs forty cents.
¿A cómo se vende el kilo de café?	How much is a kilo of coffee?
Se vende a trescientas pesetas el kilo.	It costs three hundred pesetas a kilo.

B. IT COSTS . . .

Cuesta . . .	It costs . . .
Este libro cuesta tres mil pesos.	This book costs three thousand pesos.

Compró un coche por diez mil dólares.
He bought a car for ten thousand dollars.

He ahorrado setenta y dos dólares para comprarme un vestido.
I've saved seventy-two dollars to buy clothing.

En el mes de junio hizo treinta y cinco mil ochocientos veintidós pesos.
He made 35,822 pesos in the month of June.

Se vende solamente por kilos, y cuesta cien pesos el kilo.
It's sold only by the kilo and costs one hundred pesos per kilo.

C. MY ADDRESS IS . . .

Yo vivo en el doscientos cincuenta de la calle Rivadavia.
I live at 250 Rivadavia Street.

Ella vive en el trescientos del Paseo de la Gracia.
She lives at 300 Paseo de la Gracia.

La tienda queda en el trescientos veintiséis de la Avenida de Mayo.
The store is at 326 May Avenue.

Se trasladaron a la Plaza de Colón, número novecientos veintiuno.
They moved to 921 Columbus Plaza.

D. MY TELEPHONE NUMBER IS . . .

El número de mi teléfono es el cuatro uno cinco tres dos ocho ocho.	My telephone number is 415-3288.

E. THE NUMBER IS . . .

El número es	The number is . . .
Mi número es . . .	My number is . . .
El número de mi cuarto es el treinta.	My room number is 30.
Vivo en el cuarto número treinta.	I live in room 30.
El número de mi casa es el mil trescientos veintidós.	My address ("house number") is 1322.
Vivo en el quinto piso, del trescientos treinta y dos de la Avenida Bolívar.	I live at 332 Bolivar Avenue, fifth floor.

LESSON 20

A. WHAT'S TODAY?

¿Qué día de la semana es hoy?	What's today? ("What day of the week is today?")
¿Qué día es hoy?	What day is today?
Es lunes.[1]	Monday.

[1] Refer to Lesson 6 to review the days and months.

The following expressions all mean "What's the date?":

¿A cómo estamos?	("At how are we?")
¿A cómo estamos hoy?	("At how are we today?")
¿A cuántos estamos?	("At how many are we?")
¿En qué fecha estamos?	("In what date are we?")
¿Cuál es la fecha de hoy?	What is today's date?
¿Cuál es la fecha del sábado?	What is Saturday's date?
Estamos a veinte.	It's the 20th. ("We're at the 20th.")
El primero de mayo.	The 1st of May. May 1st.
El once de abril.	The 11th of April.
El cuatro de julio.	The 4th of July.
El quince de septiembre.	The 15th of September.
El veintiuno de junio.	The 21st of June.
El veinticinco de diciembre.	The 25th of December.
El diecisiete de noviembre.	The 17th of November.
El trece de febrero.	The 13th of February.
El veintiocho de agosto.	The 28th of August.

B. SOME DATES

Don Quijote fue publicado en mil seiscientos cinco.	"Don Quixote" was published in 1605.

Shakespeare y Cervantes murieron en mil seiscientos dieciséis.	Shakespeare and Cervantes both died in 1616.
Su padre murió en mil novecientos setenta y cinco.	His father died in 1975.
Estuvimos allí en mil novecientos ochenta o mil novecientos ochenta y uno.	We were there in 1980 or 1981.
¿Qué sucedió en mil novecientos ochenta y nueve.	What happened in 1989?
Cayó la muralla de Berlín en el mil novecientos ochenta y nueve.	The Berlin Wall fell in 1989.

C. To Go: *IR*

The forms of this verb are irregular; they do not follow a set pattern.

1. I go

yo voy	I go
tú vas	you go
él va	he goes
nosotros vamos	we go
vosotros vais	you go
ellos van	they go

2. I'm not going

no voy	I'm not going
no vas	you're not going
no va	he's not going
no vamos	we're not going
no vais	you're not going
no van	they're not going

3. Study these phrases:

Vamos a la playa el lunes.	We're going to the beach Monday.
¿Cuándo vas al mercado?	When are you going to the market?
Voy ahora.	I'm going now.
¡Vamos!	Let's go!
¡Me voy!	I'm going (leaving)!
Van al cine el martes.	They're going to the movies Tuesday.
Voy a ir a Santiago en diciembre.	I'm going to go to Santiago in December.
Vamos a comer.	We're going to eat.
¡Vaya!	Well! How about that! ("Go!")

D. WORD STUDY

conclusión	conclusion
condición	condition
consideración	consideration
decisión	decision
escena	scene
estación	season

persona   person
señal   signal

QUIZ 16

1. *Es lunes.*
2. *¿A cuántos estamos?*
3. *El primero de julio.*
4. *¿En qué fecha estamos?*
5. *El once de abril.*
6. *El veintiocho de febrero.*
7. *El veinticinco de junio.*
8. *Mil seiscientos cinco.*
9. *El trece de agosto.*
10. *Fecha.*
11. *¿Qué día es hoy?*
12. *Hoy es jueves.*
13. *Van al cine.*
14. *Voy a la playa.*
15. *Vivo en el veinte de la calle Goya.*

a. The 25th of June.
b. The 28th of February.
c. The 13th of August.
d. 1605.
e. It's Monday.
f. What day of the month is it?
g. Date.
h. The first of July.
i. The 11th of April.
j. What's the date?
k. They're going to the movies.
l. I'm going to the beach.
m. I live at 20 Goya Street.
n. Today is Thursday.
o. What day is today?

ANSWERS
1—e; 2—f; 3—h; 4—j; 5—i; 6—b; 7—a; 8—d; 9—c; 10—g; 11—o; 12—n; 13—k; 14—l; 15—m.

LESSON 21

A. What Time Is It?

minuto	minute
hora	hour
¿Qué hora es?	What time is it?
Es la una.	It's 1:00.
Es la una y cinco.	It's 1:05.
Es la una y diez.	It's 1:10.
Es la una y quince.	It's 1:15.
Es la una y cuarto.	It's 1:15.
Es la una y media.	It's 1:30.
Es la una y cincuenta.	It's 1:50.
Faltan diez para las dos.	It's 1:50 ("ten minutes to two").
Son las dos.	It's 2:00.
Son las tres.	It's 3:00.
Son las cuatro.	It's 4:00.
Son las cinco.	It's 5:00.
Son las seis.	It's 6:00.
Son las siete.	It's 7:00.
Son las ocho.	It's 8:00.
Son las nueve.	It's 9:00.
Son las diez.	It's 10:00.
Son las once.	It's 11:00.
Son las tres y diez.	It's 3:10.
Son las seis y media.	It's 6:30.
Son las dos menos cuarto.	It's a quarter to two.
No son todavía las cuatro.	It's not four yet.
Es mediodía.	It's 12:00. It's noon.
Es medianoche.	It's 12:00 midnight. It's midnight.

¿Qué hora tiene usted?	What time do you have?
Mi reloj marca las cinco.	It's 5 o'clock by my watch. ("My watch marks 5 o'clock.")

Notice that for times between 1:00 and 2:00 as well as *mediodía* and *medianoche, es* is used. For all other times, *son* is used.

B. At What Time?

¿A qué hora?	At what time?
¿A qué hora sale el tren?	What time does the train leave?
A las nueve en punto.	At 9 o'clock sharp.
A eso de las nueve.	About 9 o'clock.
Hacia las nueve.	Around 9 o'clock.
A las tres menos veinte de la tarde.	At 2:40 P.M. ("twenty minutes to three").
A las seis de la tarde.	At 6 P.M.

Notice that in Spanish when you want to specify "A.M." you add *de la mañana,* for P.M., use *de la tarde* or *de la noche.*

Son las ocho de la mañana.	It's 8:00 o'clock in the morning. It's 8:00 A.M.
Son las dos de la tarde.	It's 2:00 o'clock in the afternoon. It's 2:00 P.M.

Son las nueve de la noche.
It's 9:00 in the evening. It's 9:00 P.M.

Voy al trabajo a las siete de la mañana.
I go to work at 7:00 A.M.

Voy al restaurante a las ocho de la noche.
I'm going to the restaurant at 8:00 P.M.

Notice that in Spanish "evening" begins at 7 P.M.

C. IT'S TIME

Es hora.
It's time.

Es hora de hacerlo.
It's time to do it.

Es hora de partir.[1]
It's time to leave.

Es hora de irnos a casa.
It's time for us to go home.

Tengo mucho tiempo.
I have a lot of time.

No tengo tiempo.
I haven't any time.

Está perdiendo su tiempo.
He's wasting his time.

Viene de vez en cuando.
He comes from time to time.

D. TIME EXPRESSIONS

hace dos minutos   two minutes ago
hace tres horas   three hours ago
en media hora   in a half hour
después de las ocho   after 8:00
antes de las nueve   before 9:00
a tiempo   on time
temprano   early
tarde   late

[1] Or you might choose to say: *Es hora de salir.*

QUIZ 17

1. *Es hora de hacerlo.*	a. He comes from time to time.
2. *¿Qué hora es?*	b. It's 9:00.
3. *Es la una.*	c. At what time?
4. *Son las tres.*	d. It's time to do it.
5. *Son las nueve.*	e. It's 2:00.
6. *Es medianoche.*	f. It's 1:00.
7. *¿A qué hora?*	g. I haven't any time.
8. *No tengo tiempo.*	h. It's 2:40 p.m. ("twenty minutes to 3").
9. *Es la una y cuarto.*	i. It's noon.
10. *Son las cuatro.*	j. It's 3:00.
11. *Son las dos.*	k. It's 1:05.
12. *Viene de vez en cuando.*	l. It's 4:00.
13. *Es mediodía.*	m. What time is it?
14. *Es la una y cinco.*	n. It's 1:15.
15. *Son las tres menos veinte de la tarde.*	o. It's midnight.

ANSWERS
1—d; 2—m; 3—f; 4—j; 5—b; 6—o; 7—c; 8—g; 9—n; 10—l; 11—e; 12—a; 13—i; 14—k; 15—h.

LESSON 22

A. YESTERDAY, TODAY, TOMORROW, ETC.

PASADO	PRESENTE	FUTURO
ayer	**hoy**	**mañana**
yesterday	today	tomorrow

ayer por la mañana	esta mañana	mañana por la mañana
yesterday morning	this morning	tomorrow morning
ayer por la tarde	esta tarde	mañana por la tarde
last evening	this evening	tomorrow evening
anoche	esta noche	mañana por la noche
last night	tonight	tomorrow night

B. Morning, Noon, Night, etc.

Esta mañana.	This morning.
Ayer por la mañana.	Yesterday morning.
Mañana por la mañana.	Tomorrow morning.
Hoy a mediodía.	This noon. Noon today.
Ayer a mediodía.	Yesterday noon.
Mañana a mediodía.	Tomorrow noon.
Esta tarde.	This evening.
Ayer por la tarde.	Yesterday evening.
Mañana por la tarde.	Tomorrow evening.
Esta noche.	Tonight.
Anoche.	Last night.
Mañana por la noche.	Tomorrow night.

C. This Week, Next Month, In a Little While, etc.

Esta semana.	This week.
La semana pasada.	Last week.

La semana que viene.	Next week.
Dentro de dos semanas.	In two weeks.
Hace dos semanas.	Two weeks ago.
Este mes.	This month.
El mes pasado.	Last month.
El mes que viene.	Next month ("the month that's coming").
Dentro de dos meses.	In two months.
Hace dos meses.	Two months ago.
El mes antepasado.	The month before last.
Este año.	This year.
El año pasado.	Last year.
El año próximo.	Next year.
El año que viene.	Next year.
Dentro de dos años.	In two years.
Hace dos años.	Two years ago.
¿Cuánto tiempo hace?	How long ago?
Hace un momento.	A moment ago ("it makes a minute").
Hace mucho tiempo.	A long time ago ("it makes much time").
Ahora.	Now.
Ahora mismo.	This very moment.
Luego, luego.	Right away. ("Later, Later.")
Por ahora.	For the time being.
En este momento.	At this moment.
De momento.	For the time being.
De un momento a otro.	At any moment.
Dentro de un momento.	In a short time.
Dentro de poco.	In a little while.
A ratos.	From time to time.

¿Cuántas veces?	How many times?
Una vez.	Once.
Cada vez.	Each time.
Dos veces.	Twice.
Rara vez.	Very seldom. Not often.
Muchas veces.	Very often.
A veces.	Sometimes.
Alguna que otra vez.	Once in a while.
De vez en cuando.	Now and then. From time to time.
Por la mañana temprano.	Early in the morning.
Al anochecer.	In the evening ("at nightfall").
Al otro día.	On the following day.
Al día siguiente.	On the following day.
De hoy en quince días.	Two weeks from today.
De hoy en ocho días.	A week from today.
De mañana en ocho días.	A week from tomorrow.
Dentro de una semana.	In a week.
El miércoles de la semana que viene.	Next Wednesday.
El lunes de la semana pasada.	Monday a week ago.
El cinco del corriente.	The fifth of this month.
El cinco del mes pasado.	The fifth of last month.
A principios de marzo.	At the beginning of March.
A fin de mes.	At the end of the month.
A principios de año.	In the early part of the year.

A fines de año.　　　Toward the end of the
　　　　　　　　　　　　year.

Pasó hace ocho años.　It happened eight years
　　　　　　　　　　　　ago.

QUIZ 18

1. *Ayer por la*　　　　　a. Last year.
   mañana.
2. *Esta tarde.*　　　　　b. Last night.
3. *Mañana por la*　　　　c. Today at noon.
   tarde.
4. *Anoche.*　　　　　　　d. Now.
5. *El mes que viene.*　　e. In two weeks.
6. *Ahora.*　　　　　　　f. In a little while.
7. *La semana pasada.*　g. Yesterday morning.
8. *El año pasado.*　　　h. From time to time.
9. *Hoy a mediodía.*　　i. It happened eight
　　　　　　　　　　　　　years ago.
10. *Dentro de poco.*　　j. This afternoon.
11. *Esta semana.*　　　　k. Sometimes.
12. *Pasó hace ocho*　　　l. Within a week.
    años.
13. *A fines de año.*　　m. Tomorrow afternoon.
14. *Hace dos meses.*　　n. Next month.
15. *A fines de mes.*　　o. Last week.
16. *Dentro de una*　　　p. Each time.
    semana.
17. *A ratos.*　　　　　q. About the end of
　　　　　　　　　　　　　the month.
18. *A veces.*　　　　　r. Towards the end of
　　　　　　　　　　　　　the year.
19. *Dentro de dos*　　　s. This week.
    semanas.
20. *Cada vez.*　　　　　t. Two months ago.

ANSWERS
1—g; 2—j; 3—m; 4—b; 5—n; 6—d; 7—o; 8—a;
9—c; 10—f; 11—s; 12—i; 13—r; 14—t; 15—q;
16—l; 17—h; 18—k; 19—e; 20—p.

REVIEW QUIZ 4

1. *Compró un coche por* _____ (four thousand)
   dólares.
   a. *tres mil*
   b. *cuatrocientos*
   c. *cuatro mil*

2. *Su número de teléfono es* _____ (845-0860).
   a. *ocho, dos, seis, cinco, cero, seis, nueve*
   b. *seis, cinco, tres, seis, nueve, dos, cero*
   c. *ocho, cuatro, cinco, cero, ocho, seis, cero*

3. *¿En qué* _____ (date) *estamos?*
   a. *día*
   b. *mes*
   c. *fecha*

4. *¿A cómo estamos* _____ (today)?
   a. *mes*
   b. *hoy*
   c. *cómo*

5. *El* _____ (17) *de diciembre.*
   a. *diecisiete*
   b. *veintisiete*
   c. *quince*

6. *Es la* _____ (1:10).
   a. *una y cinco*
   b. *una y diez*
   c. *una y cuarto*

7. *Son las* _____ (7:00).
   a. *siete*
   b. *nueve*
   c. *seis*

8. *Es* _____ (12:00 noon).
   a. *medianoche*
   b. *mediodía*
   c. *once*

9. *A las* _____ (2:40).
   a. *falta un cuarto para las cuatro*
   b. *tres menos veinte*
   c. *una y cuarenticinco*

10. _____ (yesterday) *por la mañana.*
    a. *hoy*
    b. *ayer*
    c. *esta*

11. *La* _____ (week) *pasada.*
    a. *semana*
    b. *noche*
    c. *mañana*

12. *Dentro de un* _____ (in a little while).
    a. *rato*
    b. *día*
    c. *poco*

13. *Hace dos* _____ (years).
    a. *meses*
    b. *años*
    c. *días*

14. *El* _____ (Wednesday) *de la semana que viene.*
    a. *lunes*
    b. *viernes*
    c. *miércoles*

15. *A* _____ (end) *del año.*
    a. *fines*
    b. *principios*
    c. *primeros*

ANSWERS
1—c; 2—c; 3—c; 4—b; 5—a; 6—b; 7—a; 8—b;
9—b; 10—b; 11—a; 12—c; 13—b; 14—c; 15—a.

D. WORD STUDY

adelanto	advance (noun)
banco	bank
capítulo	chapter
contenido	content
delicioso	delicious
enemigo	enemy
fruta	fruit
millón	million
permanencia	permanence
rico	rich

LESSON 23

A. No, Nothing, Never, Nobody

The word for "not"—*no*—comes before the conjugated verb:

No veo.	I don't see.
Usted no ve.	You don't see.

There are two forms for "nothing," "never," "nobody," etc.—one with and one without *no:*

No veo nada.	I see nothing. I don't see anything.
No voy nunca.	I never go.
No viene nadie por aquí.	No one is coming here. Nobody comes here.

Or—

Nada veo.	I see nothing. I don't see anything.
Nunca voy.	I never go.
Nadie viene.	No one is coming.
Sí, señor.	Yes sir.
No, señor.	No, sir.
Dice que sí.	He says yes.
Dice que no.	He says no.
Creo que sí.	I think so.
No está bien.	It's not good.
No está mal.	It's not bad.
No es eso.	It's not that.
No está aquí.	He's not here.
Aquí está.	It's here.

No es mucho.	It's not a lot./mucn.
No es suficiente.	It's not enough.
Es bastante.	It's enough.
No tan de prisa.	Not so fast.
No tan a menudo.	Not so often.
No es nada.	It's nothing.
Eso no es nada.	That's nothing.
No es gran cosa.	It's not very important.
No tengo tiempo.	I have no time.
No sé cómo ni cuándo.	I don't know how or when.
No sé dónde.	I don't know where.
No sé nada.	I don't know anything.
No sé nada de eso.	I know nothing about it.
No quiero nada.	I don't want anything.
Nada quiero.	I don't want anything.
No importa.	It doesn't matter. It's not important.
No me importa.	I don't care. It makes no difference to me.
No me importa nada.	I don't care at all. It doesn't make the slightest difference to me.
No lo diga.	Don't say it.
¡No me diga!	You don't say!
No tengo nada que decir.	I've nothing to say.
Nunca lo diré.	I'll never say it.
No ha pasado nada.	Nothing happened.
No tengo nada que hacer.	I have nothing to do.
Nunca lo veo.	I never see him.

Nunca lo he visto.	I've never seen him before.
Jamás lo he visto.	I've never seen him before.
Nunca viene.	He never comes.
Jamás ha venido.	He has never come.
Nunca voy.	I never go.
Jamás iré.	I'll never go.

B. NEITHER, NOR

Ni.
Nor.

No he dicho ni una palabra.
I haven't said a word.

Ni . . . ni.
Neither . . . nor.

Ni más ni menos.
Just so ("neither more nor less").

Ni el uno ni el otro.
Neither the one nor the other.

Ni esto ni aquello.
Neither this one nor that one over there.

Ni tanto ni tan poco.
Neither too much nor too little.

No es bueno ni malo.
It's so-so. It's not too good and not too bad.

No puedo ni quiero ir.
I can't go and I don't want to.

No tengo ni tiempo ni dinero.
I have neither the time nor the money.

No sabe leer ni escribir.
He can neither read nor write.

No tengo cigarrillos ni fósforos.
I haven't any cigarettes or matches.

C. WORD STUDY

ángulo	angle
calidad	quality
causa	cause
convicción	conviction
distancia	distance
efecto	effect
instante	instant
oscuro	obscure
proprietario	proprietor

LESSON 24

A. ISN'T IT? AREN'T THEY? ETC.

¿Verdad?
Is it?

¿No es verdad?
Isn't it?

El español es fácil, ¿no es verdad?
Spanish is easy, isn't it?

La gente aquí es muy simpática, ¿no es verdad?
The people here are very nice, aren't they?

Usted no tiene lápiz, ¿verdad?
You don't have a pencil, do you?

Usted conoce este lugar, ¿no es verdad?
You know this place, don't you?

Usted conoce al Sr.[1] Díaz, ¿no es verdad?
You know Mr. Díaz, don't you?

Usted tiene cuchara y servilleta, ¿no es verdad?
You have a spoon and a napkin, haven't you?

Usted no lleva mucho tiempo aquí, ¿verdad?
You haven't been here very long, have you?

Vendrá usted, ¿no es verdad?
You'll come, won't you?

Hace frío, ¿no es verdad?
It's cold, isn't it?

---

[1] *Sr.* is the abbreviation for *señor*.

¡Que majo! ¿Verdad?
How nice! Isn't it?

¡Que mono! ¿Verdad?
How cute! Isn't it?

Está bien, ¿verdad?
It's all right, isn't it?

B. SOME, ANY, A FEW

¿Tiene Ud. dinero?
Do you have any money?

Sí, tengo algo.
Yes, I have some.

No, no tengo nada.
No, I don't have any.

¿Tiene algún dinero?
Does he have any money?

No tiene nada.
He doesn't have any.

¿Le queda a usted algún dinero?
Do you have money left? ("Does any money remain to you?")

¿Cuántos libros tiene?
How many books do you have?

Tengo unos pocos.
I have a few.

¿Quiere Ud. algunas frutas?
Do you want some fruit?

Déme usted unas cuantas.
Give me a few.

Dénos unos cuantos.
Give us some.

Déle algunos.
Give him a few.

Algunos amigos míos.
Some of my friends.

QUIZ 19

1. *No veo.*
2. *No es nada.*
3. *Nunca lo diré.*
4. *No voy nunca.*
5. *No ve a Juan.*
6. *Creo que no.*
7. *No tan de prisa.*
8. *No sé nada.*
9. *No veo nada.*
10. *Nunca lo he visto.*
11. *No me importa.*
12. *No ha pasado nada.*
13. *Nunca viene.*
14. *No está mal.*
15. *Jamás iré.*

a. Neither this one nor that one over there.
b. I have no time.
c. Don't tell it to him.
d. Nothing happened.
e. I don't see.
f. I don't know anything.
g. I've never seen him.
h. He doesn't see John.
i. I'll never say it.
j. He never comes.
k. I see nothing.
l. I'll never go.
m. It's nothing.
n. He's not here.
o. I don't think so.

16. *No está aquí.*　　　　p. It's not bad.
17. *Nadie viene.*　　　　q. I don't care.
18. *Ni esto ni aquello.*　　r. Not so fast.
19. *No se lo diga.*　　　　s. I never go.
20. *No tengo tiempo.*　　　t. No one comes.

ANSWERS
1—e; 2—m; 3—i; 4—s; 5—h; 6—o; 7—r; 8—f;
9—k; 10—g; 11—q; 12—d; 13—j; 14—p; 15—l;
16—n; 17—t; 18—a; 19—c; 20—b.

C. LIKE, AS, HOW

Como.
Like, as, how.

Como yo.
Like me.

Como eso.
Like that.

Como esto.
Like this.

Como nosotros.
Like us.

Como los demás.
Like the others.

Éste no es como ése.
This one isn't like that one.

Así es como es.
That's how it is. That's the way it is.

Como usted quiera.
As you wish.

Es como en casa.
It's like (being) home.

No es como su padre.
He's not like his father.

Ignoro cómo explicarlo.
I don't know how to explain it.

¿Cómo es?
What does it look like? ("How is it?")

Es blanco como la nieve.
It's as white as snow.

¡Cómo llueve!
What a rain! ("How it's raining!")

¿Cómo?
What? What did you say? What do you mean?

¿Cómo no?
Why not? Yes, of course.

QUIZ 20

1. *Como usted quiera.*
2. *Como los demás.*
3. *Como esto.*

a. He's not like his father.
b. What? What did you say?
c. Give him a few.

4. *¿Tiene algún dinero?*   d. Why not?

5. *Algunos amigos míos.*   e. Do you want some fruit?

6. *No es como su padre.*   f. As you wish.

7. *¿Cómo?*   g. Does he have any money? Do you have money?

8. *Déle algunos.*   h. Like the others.

9. *¿Cómo no?*   i. Like this.

10. *¿Quiere usted algo de fruta?*   j. Some of my friends.

ANSWERS
1—f; 2—h; 3—i; 4—g; 5—j; 6—a; 7—b; 8—c; 9—d; 10—e.

LESSON 25

Let's review some greetings and introductions.

A. HAVE YOU TWO MET?

¿Conoce usted a mi amigo?
Do you know my friend?

Creo que ya nos hemos conocido.
I believe we've met before.

No creo que haya tenido el gusto.
I don't believe I've had the pleasure.

No tengo el gusto de conocerle.
I haven't had the pleasure ("of meeting you").

¿Conoces a mi amigo?
Do you know my friend *(fam.)?*

¡Por supuesto!
Of course!

Creo que ustedes ya se conocen, ¿verdad?
I think you already know one another. ("I believe you already know one another, don't you?")

Claro que nos conocemos.
Of course we know one another.

No tengo el gusto.
I haven't had the pleasure.

Ya he tenido el gusto de conocerlo.
I've already had the pleasure of meeting him.

Quisiera presentarle a Juana.
I'd like to introduce you to Joan.

Permítame que le presente a mi amigo Antonio de Alarcón.
Allow me to introduce you to my friend, Antonio de Alarcón.

B. HELLO, HOW ARE YOU?

Buenos días.
Good morning. Good afternoon. Good day.

Muy buenos días.
("A very") Good morning.

¡Hola!
Hello! Hi!

¿Cómo le va?
How are you getting along *(pol.)*?

¿Cómo te va?
How are you getting along *(fam.)*?

Regular. ¿Y a usted?
So-so. And you *(pol.)*?

¿Y a ti?
And you *(fam.)*?

¿Y a usted cómo le va?
And how are you getting along *(pol.)*?

¿Y a ti cómo te va?
And how are you getting along *(fam.)*?

¿Qué hay de nuevo?
What's new?

Nada de particular.
Nothing much.

Poca cosa.
Nothing much.

¿Qué tal te encuentras?
How are you *(fam.)*?

Aquí estamos.
I'm fine.

¿Hay algo de nuevo?
("Is there") Anything new?

No hay nada de nuevo.
There's nothing new.

¿Qué le pasa que no se le ve?
Where have you been? ("What has happened that no
   one sees you?")

He estado muy ocupado estos días.
I've been very busy these days.

No deje de telefonearme de vez en cuando.
Give me a ring once in a while.

Le telefonearé un día de estos.
I'll phone you one of these days.

¿Por qué no viene por casa?
Why don't you come to see us ("to our house")?

Iré a visitarlos la semana que viene.
I'll call on you next week. ("I'll come to visit you.")

Que no se le olvide lo prometido.
Now don't forget your ("the") promise.

Entonces hasta la semana que viene.
Until next week then.

LESSON 26

A.   Glad to Have Met You

Me alegro mucho de conocerlo.
Glad (happy) to have met you.

Encantado.
Glad to have met you ("Charmed.").

Espero volver a verlo pronto.
Hope to see you again soon.

Así lo espero yo.
I hope so ("So do I hope it.").

Aquí tiene usted mis señas y mi teléfono.
Here's my address and telephone number.

¿Tiene usted mis señas?
Do you have my address?

No, démelas usted.
No, let me have it.

Notice that the feminine plural form *las* is used because it refers to the feminine plural noun *las señas*.

Aquí las tiene.
Here it is.

Muchas gracias.
Thanks.

Se hace tarde.
It's getting late.

Es hora de regresar.
It's time to get back.

Nos vamos mañana.
We're leaving tomorrow.

¿Cuándo puedo telefonear a usted?
When can I phone you?

Por la mañana.
In the morning.

Esperaré su llamada.
I'll be expecting your call.

B. So Long

Hasta pronto.
So long/See you soon.

Hasta más tarde.
See you later.

Hasta la vista.
So long/See you soon.

Hasta luego.
So long. See you later.

Hasta otro rato.
So long. See you again ("until another time").

Hasta mañana.
See you tomorrow ("till tomorrow").

Hasta el sábado.
See you Saturday ("till Saturday").

Hasta la semana que viene.
See you next week ("till next week").

Adiós.
Good-bye.

QUIZ 21

1. *Espero volver a verlo pronto.*	a. Do you have my address?
2. *Adiós.*	b. See you tomorrow.
3. *Me alegro mucho de conocerlo.*	c. How are you getting along?
4. *¿Tiene usted mis señas?*	d. Until Saturday.
5. *Encantado.*	e. Do you know my friend?
6. *¿Conoce usted a mi amigo?*	f. Glad to have met you.
7. *Hasta mañana.*	g. Thanks a lot.
8. *¿Cómo le va?*	h. Hope to see you soon.
9. *Muchas gracias.*	i. Glad to have met you.
10. *Hasta el sábado.*	j. Good-bye.

ANSWERS
1—h; 2—j; 3—f; 4—a; 5—i; 6—e; 7—b; 8—c; 9—g;
10—d.

C. VISITING SOMEONE

¿Vive aquí el señor Santiago Navarro?
Does Mr. Santiago Navarro live here?

Aquí vive.
Yes, he does. ("He lives here.")

¿En qué piso?
On what floor?

Tercero izquierda.
Third floor left.

¿Está en casa el señor García?
Is Mr. Garcia at home?

No, señor. Ha salido.
No, sir. He's gone out.

¿A qué hora volverá?
What time will he be back?

No se lo puedo decir.
I can't tell you.

¿Desea dejarle un recado?
Do you want to leave him a message?

Si, necesito decirle algo.
Yes, I need to tell him something.

Le dejaré una nota, si me permite un lápiz y un papel.
I'll leave him a note, if I may borrow ("if you will permit me") a pencil and a sheet of paper from you.

Volveré más tarde.
I'll come back later.

Volveré por la noche.
I'll come back at night.

Volveré mañana.
I'll come back tomorrow.

Volveré otro día.
I'll come back another day.

Estaré en casa todo el día.
I'll be at home all day.

Voy al correo.
I'm going to the post office.

¿Dónde venden sellos?
Where are stamps sold?

¿Tiene usted sellos?
Do you have stamps?

Necesito un sello para el correo aéreo.
I need an airmail stamp.

Aquí hay sellos.
Here are some stamps.

Un sello de urgencia, por favor.
A special delivery stamp, please.

¿Dónde está el buzón?
Where is the mailbox?

QUIZ 22

1. *Tercero izquierda.*
2. *Volveré más tarde.*
3. *¿Vive aquí el señor Santiago Navarro?*
4. *Voy al correo.*

5. *Volveré por la noche.*
6. *Ha salido.*
7. *¿Qué piso?*
8. *Le dejaré una nota.*
9. *Estaré en casa todo el día.*
10. *No se lo puedo decir.*

a. I'll be at home all day.
b. He's gone out.
c. I'll come back tonight.
d. I can't tell you.
e. What floor?
f. I'll leave him a note.
g. I'm going to the post office.
h. Does Mr. Santiago Navarro live here?
i. Third floor left.
j. I'll come back later.

ANSWERS
1—i; 2—j; 3—h; 4—g; 5—c; 6—b; 7—e; 8—f;
9—a; 10—d.

D. WORD STUDY

ambición	ambition
brillante	brilliant
capital	capital
contacto	contact
departamento	department
mamá	mama
monumento	monument
obstáculo	obstacle
reciente	recent

LESSON 27

A. PLEASE

Por favor.
Please.

Haga usted el favor de ...
Please ("Do the favor of ") ...

Haga usted el favor de entrar.
Please come in.

Haga el favor de llevar esto.
Please carry this.

Hágame usted el favor de venir.
Please come ("Do me the favor of coming.").

Háganos usted el favor de entrar.
Please come in ("Do us the favor of entering.").

Hagan ustedes el favor de entrar.
Please come in (speaking to several people).

¿Nos hacen ustedes el favor de esperar un ratito?
Will you please wait a short while?

¿Me hace el favor de llamar un taxi?
Will you please call a taxi?

Tenga la bondad.
Please ("have the goodness").

**Tenga la bondad de decirme dónde queda la
   estación.**
Please tell me where the station is.

Su boleto, por favor.
Your ticket, please.

Siéntese aquí, por favor.
Please sit here.

Sírvase.
Please.

Sírvase hacerlo lo más pronto posible.
Please do it as soon as possible.

Sírvase decirme dónde está la biblioteca.
Please tell me where the library is.

B.   EXCUSE ME, I'M SORRY

Perdón.
Pardon me. Excuse me.

Perdóneme.
Pardon me.

Dispénseme.
Excuse me.

Disculpe.
Excuse me. Sorry.

Dispense usted.
Excuse me. Pardon me.

Dispense mi atraso.
Excuse my lateness.

Con permiso.
Excuse me.

Lo siento.
I'm sorry.

Lo siento mucho.
I'm so sorry.

Le tengo lástima.
I feel sorry for him.

QUIZ 23

1. *Siéntese aquí, por favor.*
2. *Hágame usted el favor de venir.*
3. *¿Me hace usted el favor de llamar un taxi?*
4. *Dispense mi atraso.*
5. *Dispense usted.*
6. *Haga usted el favor de entrar.*
7. *Tenga la bondad de decirme dónde queda la estación.*
8. *Haga el favor de llevar esto.*
9. *Lo siento.*
10. *Sírvase decirme dónde está la biblioteca.*

a. Excuse my lateness.
b. Excuse me. Pardon me.
c. Please come.
d. Please carry this.
e. Please tell me where the library is.
f. I'm sorry.
g. Will you please call a taxi?
h. Please come in.

  i. Please tell me where the station is.
  j. Please sit here.

ANSWERS
1—j; 2—c; 3—g; 4—a; 5—b; 6—h; 7—i; 8—d;
9—f; 10—e.

C. SOME USEFUL VERBAL EXPRESSIONS

  1. *Acabar de* means "to have just":

Acaba de llegar.
He just came.

Acabo de terminar mi trabajo.
I've just finished my work.

Juan acababa de salir cuando yo llegué.
John had just gone out when I came (arrived).

  2. *Tener que* means "to have to":

Tengo que ir.	I have to go.
Tengo que irme.	I have to leave.

Tiene que estudiar.
You have to study.

¡Tenemos que comer!
We have to eat!

  3. *Hay* means "there is" or "there are":

Hay mucha gente aquí.
There are a lot of people here.

Hay un hotel cerca de aquí.
There is a hotel near here.

4. *Quisiera* means "I would like to"; it's a more polite or formal form for "I want," *Quiero*.

Quisiera sentarme aquí.
I would like to sit here.

Quisiera presentarle a . . .
I'd like to introduce you to . . .

Quisiera ir pero no puedo.
I'd like to go but I can't.

REVIEW QUIZ 5

1. *¿Está en _____ (home, house) el señor Navarro?*
   a. *piso*
   b. *hora*
   c. *casa*

2. *¿Desea dejarle un _____ (message)?*
   a. *lápiz*
   b. *recado*
   c. *papel*

3. *¿Dispense mi _____ (lateness).*
   a. *llevar*
   b. *favor*
   c. *atraso*

4. _____ (I need) *decirle algo.*
    a. *Venden*
    b. *Necesito*
    c. *Urgencia*

5. *No veo* _____ (nothing).
    a. *a nadie*
    b. *nada*
    c. *nunca*

6. *No viene* _____ (nobody).
    a. *nadie*
    b. *nada*
    c. *nunca*

7. *No sabe leer* _____ (nor) *escribir.*
    a. *no*
    b. *ni*
    c. *jamás*

8. *El español es fácil* _____ (isn't it)?
    a. *¿es como*
    b. *¿nada*
    c. *¿verdad*

9. *Tenga la* _____ *de decirme dónde queda la estación.*
    a. *dispense*
    b. *bondad*
    c. *haga*

10. *Hagan ustedes el* _____ *de entrar.*
    a. *bondad*
    b. *favor*
    c. *sírvase*

11. _____ (Please) *hacerlo lo más pronto posible.*
    a. *Sírvase*
    b. *Dispense*
    c. *Favor*

12. _____ (I've just) *de terminar mi trabajo.*
    a. *Llegar*
    b. *Acabo*
    c. *Acaba*

13. _____ (I would like) *ir pero no puedo.*
    a. *Quisiera*
    b. *Acaba*
    c. *Quiero*

14. *Tengo* _____ *salir ahora.*
    a. *por*
    b. *que*
    c. *en*

15. *No es* _____ (like) *su padre.*
    a. *como*
    b. *cómo*
    c. *algunos*

ANSWERS
1—c; 2—b; 3—c; 4—b; 5—b; 6—a; 7—b; 8—c;
9—b; 10—b; 11—a; 12—b; 13—a; 14—b; 15—a.

D. WORD STUDY

bola, pelota	ball
rechazo	check
civil	civil
educación	education

esfuerzo	effort
lógico	logical
mesa	table
omisión	omission
página	page

LESSON 28

A. WHO? WHAT? WHEN? ETC.

1. *¿Quién?* "Who?"

¿Quién es?	Who is he (she)?
No sé quién es.	I don't know who he is.
¿Quiénes son?	Who are they?
¿Quién lo ha dicho?	Who said it?
¿Quién ha dicho eso?	Who said so?
¿Quién lo ha hecho?	Who did it?
¿De quién es este lápiz?	Whose pencil is this?
¿Para quién es esto?	Who is this for?
¿A quién quiere ver usted?	Who(m) do you wish to see?
¿Quién sabe?	Who knows?
¿A quién pertenece esto?	Whose is this?

2. *¿Qué?* "What?"

¿Qué es esto?	What's this?
¿Qué es eso?	What's that?
¿Qué pasa?	What's the matter? What's up?
¿Qúe sucede?	What's the matter? What's up?

¿Qué sucedió?	What happened?
¿Qué hay de nuevo?	What's new?
¿Qué le parece?	What do you think?
¿Qué son?	What are they?
¿Qué tienen ustedes?	What do you have? What's the matter with you?
¿Qué hora es?	What time is it?
¿Qué dice usted?	What are you saying?
¿Qué ha dicho usted?	What did you say?
¿De qué hablan ustedes?	What are you talking about?
¿De qué se trata?	What's it all about? What's the point?
¿Qué quiere?	What do you want?
¿Qué desea usted?	What can I do for you? What do you wish?

3. *¿Por qué?* "Why?"

¿Por qué así?	Why so?
¿Por qué no?	Why not?
¿Por qué razón?	For what reason?
¿Por qué lo dice usted?	Why do you say that?
¿Por qué tanta prisa?	Why are you in such a hurry? Why the hurry?
¿Por qué lo ha hecho usted?	Why did you do it?

4. *¿Cómo?* "How?"

¿Cómo se dice en español esto?	How do you say this in Spanish?
¿Cómo se llama usted?	What is your name? ("How do you call yourself?")
¿Cómo se escribe eso?	How is that written (spelled)?

5. *¿Cuánto?* "How Much?"

¿Cuánto dinero necesita usted?	How much money do you need?
¿Cuántos libros hay?	How many books are there?

6. *¿Cuál?* "What?" "Which?"

¿Cuál es su nombre?	What is his name?
¿Cuál quiere usted?	Which (one) do you want?
¿Cuál quiere, éste o aquél?	Which (one) do you want, this or that one?
¿Cuál de estos lápices es de usted?	Which one of these pencils is yours?
¿Cuál de los dos caminos conduce a Madrid?	Which of these two roads leads to Madrid?

7. *¿Dónde?* "Where?"

¿Dónde está su amigo?	Where is your friend?
¿Dónde vive él?	Where does he live?
¿Dónde estás?	Where are you?
¿Dónde está la parada de autobuses?	Where is the bus stop?

8. *¿Cuándo?* "When?"

¿Cuándo vendrá su hermano?	When will your brother come?
¿Cuándo ocurrió eso?	When did that happen?

¿Cuándo se marcha usted?	When are you going (leaving)?
No sé cuándo.	I don't know when.
¿Hasta cuándo?	Until when? How long?
No sé hasta cuándo.	I don't know until when. I don't know how long.
¿Para cuándo?	How soon?
Para cuando usted quiera.	As soon as you like.
¿Desde cuándo?	Since when?
¿Desde cuándo acá?	Since when? How come? How's that?

QUIZ 24

1. *¿Cómo se llama usted?*
2. *¿Cuántos libros hay?*
3. *¿Cómo se dice esto en español?*
4. *¿Qué dice usted?*
5. *¿Cuándo ocurrió eso?*
6. *¿Desde cuándo?*
7. *¿Quién sabe?*
8. *¿Por qué no?*
9. *¿Dónde vive él?*
10. *¿Cómo se escribe eso?*

a. When did that happen?
b. Since when?
c. Who knows?
d. Where does he live?
e. What's your name?
f. What are you saying?
g. Why not?
h. How is this writen?
i. How many books are there?
j. How do you say this in Spanish?

ANSWERS
1—e; 2—i; 3—j; 4—f; 5—a; 6—b; 7—c; 8—g; 9—d; 10—h.

B. WHAT A SURPRISE! WHAT A PITY! HOW AWFUL! HOW NICE!

¡Qué sorpresa!	What a surprise!
¡Vaya!	Well! How about that!
¡Qué lástima!	What a pity!
Es una lástima.	It's a pity.
¡Qué va!	No way! What baloney!
¡Qué tontería!	How stupid! What stupidity!
¡Qué bobada!	What nonsense!
¡Qué lata!	What a drag!
¡Qué suerte!	How lucky! What luck!
¡Qué suerte loca!	What unbelievable ("crazy") luck!
¡Qué desgracia!	How unfortunate! What a misfortune!
¡Qué horror!	How awful! What a horror!
¡Qué bueno!	How nice!
¡Qué bonito!	How pretty! How nice!
¡Qué lindo!	How pretty!
¡Qué hermoso!	How beautiful!

REVIEW QUIZ 6

1. *¡Qué* _____ (unfortunate)!
    a. *suerte*
    b. *desgracia*
    c. *lástima*

2. *¡Qué* _____ (nice)!
    a. *bonito*
    b. *suerte*
    c. *lata*

3. _____ (There is) *un hotel aquí.*
    a. *Acaba*
    b. *Tienen*
    c. *Hay*

4. *Tengo* _____ (a few).
    a. *unos pocos*
    b. *algo*
    c. *como*

5. *Déme usted unos* _____ (a few).
    a. *nada*
    b. *cuantos*
    c. *algo*

6. *Quiere usted* _____ (some) *de fruta?*
    a. *algunos*
    b. *cuantos*
    c. *algo*

7. _____ (Give me) *unas cuantas.*
    a. *Déme*
    b. *Tengo mis*
    c. *Dénos*

8. *He estado muy* _____ (busy) *estos días.*
    a. *siempre*
    b. *ocupado*
    c. *nuevo*

9. *¿Se* _____ (know) *ustedes?*
    a. *conocido*
    b. *conocen*
    c. *conocerlo*

10. *¿Con quién tengo el gusto de* _____ (speak)?
    a. *hablar*
    b. *tengo*
    c. *conocer*

11. *Aquí tiene usted mis* _____ (address) *y mi telé-fono.*
    a. *día*
    b. *tarjeta*
    c. *señas*

12. *A ver si nos vemos un* _____ (day) *de estos.*
    a. *día*
    b. *muy*
    c. *semana*

13. *Hasta* _____ (later).
    a. *mañana*
    b. *más tarde*
    c. *lugar*

14. *¿*_____ (What) *dice usted?*
    a. *Cómo*
    b. *Cuándo*
    c. *Qué*

15. *¿*_____ (Why) *se fue ella?*
    a. *Qué*
    b. *Por qué*
    c. *Cuánto*

16. *¿*_____ (How) *se dice esto en español?*
    a. *Cómo*
    b. *Cuándo*
    c. *Nadie*

17. ¿_____ (How much) *dinero necesita usted?*
    a. *Quién*
    b. *Cuánto*
    c. *Cuyo*

18. ¿_____ (Who) *vino con usted?*
    a. *Quién*
    b. *Cuyo*
    c. *Cuál*

19. ¿_____ (Where) *está su amigo?*
    a. *Dónde*
    b. *Cómo*
    c. *Qué*

20. ¿_____ (When) *vendrá su hermano?*
    a. *Quién*
    b. *Cuál*
    c. *Cuándo*

ANSWERS
1—b; 2—a; 3—c; 4—a; 5—b; 6—c; 7—a; 8—b;
9—b; 10—a; 11—c; 12—a; 13—b; 14—c; 15—b;
16—a; 17—b; 18—a; 19—a; 20—c.

C. WORD STUDY

angustioso	anxious
jefe	chief
dificultad	difficulty
doctor	doctor
episodio	episode
futuro	future
glorioso	glorious
nervioso	nervous
periodo	period

LESSON 29

A. IT'S GOOD

Bueno.	Good.
Muy bueno.	Very good.
Es muy bueno.	It's very good.
Es excelente.	It's excellent.
Es estupendo.	It's wonderful.
Es magnífico.	It's excellent. It's wonderful.
Es admirable.	It's excellent. It's admirable.
Es perfecto.	It's perfect.
Está bien.	It's all right.
No está mal.	It's not bad.
¿Está bien esto?	Is it all right?
¡Muy bien!	Very well! Very good!
Es bella.	She's beautiful.
Es bellísima.	She's very beautiful.
Es muy linda.	She's very pretty.
Es encantador.	He's charming.
Es buen tipo, ¡vaya!	He's a really good guy!
¡Es buena onda!	He's a good guy! He's a good egg!

B. IT'S NOT GOOD

No es bueno.	It's not good/It's no good.
Es malo.	It's bad.
No es muy bueno.	It's not very good.
Eso no es bueno.	That's no good.

Esto no está bien.[1]	It's not right. This isn't right. This isn't proper. This is wrong.
Eso es malo.	That's bad.
Es bastante malo.	It's (he's) very bad.
Eso es pésimo.	That's bad. That's awfully bad.
Eso es malísimo.	That's very bad.
Es verdaderamente malo.	He's (it's) really ("truly") bad.
¡Es tonto!	It's silly. It's stupid.
No me interesa.	I don't care for it. It doesn't interest me.
Eso no vale nada.	That's worthless.
No vale la pena.	It's not worth the trouble. It's not worth it. ("It's not worth the pain.")
No sirve para nada.	It's worthless. It's good for nothing.
¡Qué lástima!	What a pity!
¡Qué desgracia!	How unfortunate! ("What a misfortune!")
¡Qué horror!	How awful!

[1] In general, *bien* is used as an adverb meaning "well." It is most often used after a verb, as in *Entiendo bien el español*. I understand Spanish well.

QUIZ 25

1. *Está bien.*	a. It's excellent.
2. *Muy bien.*	b. She's very pretty.
3. *Es excelente.*	c. That's worthless!
4. *No está mal.*	d. He's a good guy!
5. *Eso es malo.*	e. That's very bad!
6. *¡Es buena onda!*	f. It's wonderful!
7. *Es muy linda.*	g. It's all right.
8. *Eso no vale nada.*	h. That's bad.
9. *¡Eso es malísimo!*	i. Very well.
10. *Es estupendo.*	j. It's not bad.

ANSWERS

1—g; 2—i; 3—a; 4—j; 5—h; 6—d; 7—b; 8—c;
9—e; 10—f.

C. I Like It

Me gusta . . .	I like . . . ("It pleases me . . .")
Me gusta.	I like it (him, her).
Me gusta mucho.	I like it (him, her) very much.
Me gusta muchísimo.	I like it (him, her) very much.
Eso me gusta.	I like that.
Ella me gusta.	I like her.
Me gustan mucho.	I like them a lot.
¿Le gusta?	Do you like it?
¿Le gusta a usted la fruta?	Do you like fruit?
Sí, me gusta la fruta.	Yes, I like fruit.
¿Les gusta el chocolate?	Do you *(pl.)* like chocolate?

¿Le gusta América?	Do you like America?
¿Le gustan los Estados Unidos?	Do you like the United States?
¿Le gusta la comida española?	Do you like Spanish food?
¿Le gusta España?	Do you like Spain?
¿Le gustó España?	Did you like Spain?
Me gustó España.	I liked Spain.
¿Te gusta?	Do you like it *(fam.)*?
¿Te gustan?	Do you like them?
¿Te gusta viajar?	Do you like to travel?
¿Cree que les gustará la casa?	Do you think they'll like the house?
¿Cómo les gusta mi cuarto?	How do you *(pl.)* like my room?
Me gusta.	I like it.
Me gusta mucho.	I like it very much.
Si a usted le gusta.	If you like it.
Cuando usted guste.	Whenever you like.
¿Le gusta bailar?	Do you like to dance?

Notice that the Spanish for "I like fruit" is *Me gusta la fruta* ("To me is pleasing fruit"). That is, the word which is the object in English is the subject in Spanish. "I like the United States" is *Me gustan los Estados Unidos* ("To me are pleasing the United States"). Here the verb is plural because the subject is plural.

D. I Don't Like It

No me gusta.	I don't like it.
No me gusta nada.	I don't like it at all.
No me gustan esos.	I don't like those.
¿No le gusta?	Don't you like it?

¿No te gusta?	Don't you like it *(fam.)?*
¿No te gusta esta canción?	Don't you like this song *(fam.)?*
¡No me gusta bailar!	I don't like to dance!
No me interesa.	I don't care for it. It doesn't interest me.

E. I HAD A GOOD TIME!

Me he divertido mucho.	
Lo he pasado muy bien.	I had a good time.
Lo pasé muy bien.	
¡Nos divertimos como locos!	We had a terrific ("crazy") time!
Lo pasaron bien. **Se divirtieron.**	They had a good time.
¡Que se divierta!	Have a good time!

QUIZ 26

1. *¿Le gusta la comida española?*
2. *¿Le gustan?*
3. *Me gusta mucho.*
4. *¿Le gusta a usted la fruta?*
5. *Cuando usted guste.*
6. *¿Te gustó España?*
7. *¿No le gusta?*
8. *Si a usted le gusta.*
9. *No me gusta nada.*

a. I don't like it at all.
b. How do you like my room?
c. Did you like Spain?
d. If you like it.
e. Don't you like it?
f. I like it very much.
g. Do you like them?
h. Whenever you like.
i. Do you like Spanish food?

10. *¿Cómo les gusta mi   j.* Do you like fruit?
    cuarto?

ANSWERS
1—i; 2—g; 3—f; 4—j; 5—h; 6—c; 7—e; 8—d;
9—a; 10—b.

LESSON 30

A. IN, TO, FROM, ETC.[1]

Study the uses of these prepositions.

1. With Places

He estado en Madrid.	I've been in Madrid.
Voy a Madrid.	I'm going to Madrid.
Vengo de Barcelona.	I come from Barcelona.
Soy de Barcelona.	I'm from Barcelona.
Salgo para Buenos Aires.	I'm leaving for Buenos Aires.
Se dirige hacia La Paz.	He's going toward La Paz.
Llegué hasta Caracas.	I got as far as Caracas.

---

[1] In this lesson you will see some new verb tenses: the preterite, the imperfect, and the future. Be sure to refer to item C of Lesson 38, the section "The Tenses of the Verb" in the Summary of Spanish Grammar, and the verb charts for more information. For now just focus on the uses of the prepositions.

2. *A* "to," "by," "at," "on," "in"

A la derecha.	To the right.
A la izquierda.	To the left.
Dos a dos.	Two by two.
Poco a poco.	Little by little.
A pie.	On foot.
A mano.	By hand.
A mediodía.	At noon.
A medianoche.	At midnight.
Se sentaron a la mesa.	They sat down at the table.
Caminaba a la escuela.	I used to walk to school.
A la española.	In the Spanish manner.

When the direct object (of the verb) refers to a definite person or is the name of a person, *a* is used before it. This is called "the personal *a*."

Acabo de ver a mi amigo.	I have just seen my friend.
Veo a Juan.	I see John.

3. *Con* "with"

Café con leche.	Coffee with milk.
Yo fui con Juan.	I went with John.
Lo escribió con un lápiz.	He wrote it with a pencil.
Viene con María.	He's coming with Maria.
Viene conmigo.	He's coming with me.

4. *De* "of," "from"

Es de mi hermano.	It's from my brother.
Vengo de Madrid.	I come (am) from Madrid.
Es de madera.	It's made of wood.
De día.	By day. In the daytime.
De nuevo.	Again.

5. *En* "in"

Viví en México por varios años.	I lived in Mexico for several years.
Me voy en cuatro días.	I'm leaving in four days.
En lugar de.	In place of. Instead of.

6. *Hasta* "up to," "until"

Hasta Buenos Aires.	Up to (as far as) Buenos Aires.
Caminé hasta el quinto piso.	I walked up to the fifth floor.
Hasta mañana.	Until tomorrow.
Hasta luego.	See you soon. ("Until soon.")
Hasta más tarde.	See you later. ("Until later.")
Hasta la vista.	Until we see each other again.

7. *Hacia* "toward"

Hacia allí.	In that direction.
Ella caminaba hacia el parque.	She was walking toward (in the direction of) the park.

8. *Desde* "from"

Desde Barcelona hasta Madrid.	From Barcelona to Madrid.
Desde que le vi.	Since I saw him. Since the time I saw him.

9. *Sobre* "on"

Sobre la mesa.	On the table.
Tenía un pañuelo sobre la cabeza.	She had a handkerchief on her head.

10. *Por* "for," "through"

Sesenta millas por hora.	Sixty miles an hour.
Lo compré por un dólar.	I bought it for a dollar.
Le di un peso por esto.	I gave him a dollar for this.
Me dio su libro por el mío.	He exchanged books with me. He gave me his book for mine.
Pasamos por México.	We passed through Mexico.
El tren pasa por Zaragoza.	The train passes through Zaragoza.
Entró por la puerta.	He came in through the door.
Yo iré por usted.	I'll go for (in place of) you.
Fue por el médico.	He went for the doctor.
Estaré de viaje por dos años.	I'll be away traveling for two years.

11. Study these other expressions:

¿Por qué?	Why? What was the reason?
Por ahora.	For the time being.
Por la mañana.	In the morning. During the morning.
Mañana por la mañana.	Tomorrow morning.
Mañana por la tarde.	Tomorrow afternoon.
Por la tarde.	During the afternoon. In the afternoon.
Por la noche.	At night.
Pasó por la calle.	He walked along the street.
Por ejemplo.	For example.
Por consiguiente.	Consequently. As a result.
Por lo general.	In general.
Por completo.	Completely.
Por eso.	For that reason.
Por razón de . . .	By reason of . . .
Por causa de . . .	On account of . . .
Por fin.	Finally. At last.
Por aquí.	Around here.
No estoy por ir.	I'm not in favor of going.
Estoy por hacerlo.	I'm in favor of doing it.
¡Por Dios!	For goodness' sake! For heaven's sake!

12. *Para* "for" "in order to"
    Para indicates direction, purpose:

Para ir allá.	In order to go there.
Un estante para libros.	A bookcase ("a stand for books").

Salió para Tegucigalpa.	He left for Tegucigalpa.
El autobús para Lima.	The bus for Lima.
La carta es para usted.	The letter is for you.
La lección para mañana.	The lesson for tomorrow.
Para él, eso es fácil.	That's easy for him.
No sirve para nada.	It's worthless. It's good for nothing.
Estudio para ser médico.	I'm studying to be a doctor.

B. WORD STUDY

ataque	attack
aventura	adventure
cómodo	comfortable
valor	courage
independencia	independence
idioma	language
mensaje	message
opinion	opinion
silencio	silence

QUIZ 27

1. *A mediodía.*   a. On foot.
2. *Poco a poco.*   b. One by one.

3. *A la derecha.* c. I come from Madrid.
4. *A la española.* d. It's made of wood.
5. *Con.* e. By day.
6. *A pie.* f. Again.
7. *Vengo de Madrid.* g. On the table.
8. *Es de madera.* h. To the right.
9. *En cuanto a.* i. In that direction.
10. *De nuevo.* j. Little by little.
11. *Hacia allí.* k. Until tomorrow.
12. *De día.* l. At noon.
13. *A la izquierda.* m. Since I saw him.
14. *Uno a uno.* n. In the Spanish manner.
15. *Hasta Buenos Aires.* o. With.
16. *Me voy en dos días.* p. Instead of.
17. *Sobre la mesa.* q. To the left.
18. *Hasta mañana.* r. In regard to.
19. *En vez de.* s. As far as Buenos Aires.
20. *Desde que lo vi.* t. I'm leaving in two days.

ANSWERS
1—l; 2—j; 3—h; 4—n; 5—o; 6—a; 7—c; 8—d;
9—r; 10—f; 11—i; 12—e; 13—q; 14—b; 15—s;
16—t; 17—g; 18—k; 19—p; 20—m.

QUIZ 28

1. *Por ejemplo.* a. I gave him ten pesos for this.
2. *El tren pasa por Madrid.* b. Sixty miles an hour.

3. *Pasamos por México.*	c. Completely.
4. *Por ahora.*	d. For that reason.
5. *Lo compré por un dólar.*	e. Around here.
6. *Por eso.*	f. For goodness' sake!
7. *Sesenta millas por hora.*	g. At last.
8. *Por completo.*	h. For example.
9. *Le di diez pesos por esto.*	i. I'm not in favor of going.
10. *¡Por Dios!*	j. For the time being.
11. *Por fin.*	k. I bought it for a dollar.
12. *Entró por la puerta.*	l. The train passes through Madrid.
13. *Por aquí.*	m. I'll go for you.
14. *Yo iré por usted.*	n. He came in through the door.
15. *No estoy por ir.*	o. We passed through Mexico.

ANSWERS

1—h; 2—l; 3—o; 4—j; 5—k; 6—d; 7—b; 8—c; 9—a; 10—f; 11—g; 12—n; 13—e; 14—m; 15—i.

QUIZ 29

1. *La carta es para usted.*	a. A bookcase.
2. *No sirve para nada.*	b. The lesson for tomorrow.

3. *La lección para mañana.*

c. In order to go there.

4. *Está por llover.*

d. He left for Chile.

5. *Estoy por hacerlo.*

e. I'm studying to be a doctor.

6. *Un estante para libros.*

f. He's about to leave.

7. *Para ir allá.*

g. The letter is for you.

8. *Salió para Chile.*

h. I'm in favor of doing it.

9. *Está por irse.*

i. It's worthless.

10. *Estudio para médico.*

j. It's about to rain.

ANSWERS
1—g; 2—i; 3—b; 4—j; 5—h; 6—a; 7—c; 8—d; 9—f; 10—e.

LESSON 31

A. ON THE ROAD

Perdón.
Pardon me. Excuse me.

¿Cómo se llama este pueblo?
What is the name of this town?

¿A qué distancia estamos de Valparaíso?
How far are we from Valparaíso?

¿Cuántos kilómetros hay de aquí a Cali?
How many kilometers from here to Cali?

Está a diez kilómetros de aquí.
It's ten kilometers from here.

Está a veinte kilómetros de aquí.
It's twenty kilometers from here.

¿Cómo puedo ir desde aquí a Bogotá?
How do I get to Bogotá from here?

Siga este camino.
Follow this road.

¿Puede usted decirme cómo ir a esta dirección?
Can you tell me how I can get to this address?

¿Cómo se va a este lugar?
How do you get to this place?

¿Está lejos?
Is it far?

¿Cuál es el camino más corto para ir a Madrid?
What's the shortest way to get to Madrid?

¿Qué camino debo tomar?
Which road must I take?

B. WALKING AROUND

¿Tiene usted un mapa de la ciudad?
Do you have a map of the city?

¿Donde está esta calle?
Where is this street?

¿Puede usted llevarme a la calle de Alcalá?
Can you take me to Alcala Street?

¿Está cerca de aquí la calle Mayor?
Is Main Street near here?

¿Dónde hay un teléfono público?
Where is there a public phone?

¿Dónde puedo telefonear?
Where can I phone?

¿Cuántas cuadras hay de aquí a la estación?
How many blocks away is the station?

¿A qué distancia está la estación?
How far is the station?

¿Cómo se llama esta calle?
What is the name of this street?

¿Puede usted decirme dónde queda esta calle?
Can you tell me where this street is?

¿Dónde está la calle de Oro?
Where is Gold Street?

¿Está lejos de aquí?
Is it far from here?

¿Está cerca de aquí?
Is it near here?

Es la tercera cuadra a la derecha.
It's the third block to the right.

Vaya por aquí.
Go this way.

Siga todo derecho.
Go straight ahead.

Siga hasta la esquina y doble a la izquierda.
Go to the corner and turn left.

Tome la primera bocacalle a la izquierda.
Take the first intersection to the left.

¿Dónde está el garaje?
Where is the garage?

¿Dónde está la comisaría?
Where is the police station?

¿Dónde está el museo?
Where is the museum?

C. Bus, Train, Subway, Taxi

¿Dónde está la parada del autobús?
Where is the bus stop?

¿Cuánto es el pasaje?
How much is the fare?

¿En qué parada debo apearme?
What stop do I get off?

¿Dónde debo apearme?
Where do I get off?

¿Dónde está la estación del ferrocarril?
Where is the train station?

¿De qué estación sale el tren para Madrid?
From which station does the train to Madrid leave?

¿A qué estación llega el tren de Madrid?
At which station does the train from Madrid arrive?

¿Dónde está el mostrador de información?
Where is the information booth?

¿Quiere darme un horario de trenes?
Will you please let me have a train schedule?

¿Cuál es el tren para Asunción?
Which is the train for Asunción?

¿Es éste el tren de Montevideo?
Is this the train from Montevideo?

¿Dónde se toma el tren para Tucumán?
Where do you get the train for Tucumán?

En el andén número dos.
On track two.

¿A qué hora sale el tren para Madrid?
When does the train for Madrid leave?

El tren acaba de salir.
The train just left.

El tren va a salir en seguida.
The train is leaving right away.

¿A qué hora sale el próximo tren?
When does the next train leave?

¿Dónde se venden los billetes?
Where are the tickets sold?

Déme un billete de ida para Madrid.
Give me a one-way ticket to Madrid.

¿De primera o de segunda?
First or second class?

De primera.
First class.

¿Cuánto cuesta?
How much does it cost?

¿Cuánto se tarda en llegar allí?
How long does it take to get there?

¿Está ocupado este asiento?
Is this seat taken?

¿Me permite usted que ponga aquí esta maleta?
May I put this suitcase here?

¿Cuánto tiempo paramos aquí?
How long do we stop here?

¿Tengo que cambiar aquí de tren?
Do I change trains here?

¿Para este tren en Madrid?
Does this train stop in Madrid?

¿Dónde puedo comprar una ficha?
Where can I buy a token?

¿Hay un mapa del metro?
Is there a subway map?

¿Qué parada es esta?
What stop is this?

¿En qué parada debo apearme?
At what stop do I get off?

¡Taxi! ¿Está libre?
Taxi! Are you free?

Lléveme a esta dirección.
Take me to this address.

¿Qué le debo?
How much do I owe you?

QUIZ 30

1. *¿Cuál es el camino más corto para ir a . . . ?*
2. *¿Dónde puedo telefonear?*
3. *¿Dónde está esta calle?*
4. *Lléveme a esta dirección.*
5. *¿A qué distancia está la estación?*
6. *¿Me permite usar su teléfono?*
7. *¿Puede usted llevarme a la calle . . . ?*
8. *¿En qué parada debo apearme?*
9. *¿Cómo se va a este lugar?*
10. *¿Dónde está la parada del autobús?*

a. How far is the station?
b. How do you get to this place?
c. Can you take me to . . . street?
d. Where is the bus stop?
e. What stop do I get off?
f. Where can I phone?
g. Where is this street?
h. What's the shortest way to get to . . . ?
i. Take me to this address.
j. May I use your telephone?

ANSWERS
1—h; 2—f; 3—g; 4—i; 5—a; 6—j; 7—c; 8—e; 9—b;
10—d.

LESSON 32

A. Writing and Mailing Letters

Quisiera escribir una carta.
I'd like to write a letter.

¿Tiene usted un lápiz?
Do you have a pencil?

¿Tiene usted un bolígrafo?
Do you have a pen?

¿Tiene usted papel?
Do you have some paper?

¿Tiene usted un sobre?
Do you have an envelope?

¿Dónde puedo comprar un sello?
Where can I buy a stamp?

¿Dónde está el correo?
Where is the post office?

Quiero enviar esta carta.
I'd like to mail this letter.

¿Cual es el franqueo?
What is the postage (for this letter)?

¿Dónde está el buzón más cerca?
Where is the nearest mailbox?

En la esquina.
On the corner.

B. FAXES AND TELEGRAMS

Quiero enviar un fax.
I'd like to send a fax.

¿Dónde está la oficina de teléfonos?
Where is the telephone office?

Está en el centro.
It's downtown.

¿Cuánto cuesta un fax a los Estados Unidos?
How much is a fax to the United States?

Quiero enviar un telegrama.
I'd like to send a telegram.

Dónde está la oficina de telégrafos?
Where is the telegraph office?

¿Cuánto cuesta por palabra?
How much is it per word?

¿Cuánto tarda en llegar allí?
How long does it take to get there?

C. TELEPHONING

¿Hay un teléfono aquí?
Is there a phone here?

¿Dónde puedo telefonear?
Where can I phone?

¿Dónde está el teléfono?
Where is the telephone?

¿Dónde está la cabina telefónica?
Where is the phone booth?

En el vestíbulo del hotel.
In the hotel lobby.

¿Me permite usar el teléfono?
May I use your phone?

Desde luego, ¡con mucho gusto!
Of course, go ahead!

Conécteme con el servicio de larga distancia.
Give me long distance.

¿Cuánto cuesta una llamada telefónica a Madrid?
How much is a phone call to Madrid?

**Quiero hablar con el dos-dos-ocho siete-cinco-
ocho-dos.**
I want 228-7582.

Espere un momento.
Hold the wire a minute.

La línea está ocupada.
The line is busy.

Usted me dio el número equivocado.
You gave me the wrong number.

No contesta nadie.
There is no answer.

¿Puedo hablar con el señor Castro?
May I speak to Mr. Castro?

Servidor.
Speaking.

Habla el señor Villanueva.
This is Mr. Villanueva speaking.

¿El señor Castro?
Is this Mr. Castro?

El mismo.
Speaking. ("The same.")

¿Con quién hablo?
Who is this? ("With whom am I speaking?")

LESSON 33

A. What's Your Name?

¿Cómo se llama usted?
What's your name?

Me llamo Juan Castro.
My name is Juan Castro.

¿Cómo se llama él?
What's his name?

El se llama Carlos Pérez.
His name is Carlos Perez.

¿Cómo se llama ella?
What's her name?

Se llama María Fernández.
Her name is Maria Fernandez.

¿Cómo se llaman ellos?
What are their names?

El se llama José Rivera y ella Anita Ferrero.
His name is Jose Rivera and hers is Anita Ferrero.

¿Cuál es su nombre?
What's his first name?

Su nombre es Carlos.
His first name is Carlos.

¿Cuál es su apellido?
What's his last name?

Su apellido es Pérez.
His last name is Perez.

B. WHERE ARE YOU FROM?

¿De dónde es usted?
Where are you from?

Soy de Madrid.
I'm from Madrid.

¿Dónde nació usted?
Where were you born?

¿De dónde es él?
Where is he from?

Soy de Nueva York.
I'm from New York.

Es del Perú.
He's from Peru.

Nací en Madrid.
I was born in Madrid.

Ahora estoy viviendo en Barcelona.
I'm now living in Barcelona.

C. HOW OLD ARE YOU?

¿Cuántos años tiene usted?
How old are you?

Tengo veinticuatro años.
I'm twenty-four.

Cumplo veinticuatro años en septiembre.
I'll be twenty-four in September.

**Nací el diecinueve de agosto de mil novecientos
sesenta y seis.**
I was born August 19, 1966.

¿Cuándo es su cumpleaños?
When is your birthday?

**Mi cumpleaños es dentro de dos semanas, el veinti-
trés de enero.**
My birthday is in two weeks, January 23.

¿Cuántos abriles tiene?
How old is he *(fam.)*? ("How many Aprils does he
have?")

Tiene treinta abriles.
He's thirty years old.

¿Cuántos hermanos tiene usted?
How many brothers do you have?

Tengo dos hermanos.
I have two brothers.

El mayor tiene veintidós años.
The older one is twenty-two.

Estudia en la Universidad.
He studies at the University.

El menor tiene diecisiete años.
The younger one is seventeen.

Está en el último año del Instituto.
He's in his last year of high school.

¿Cuántas hermanas tiene usted?
How many sisters do you have?

Tengo una hermana.
I have one sister.

Tiene nueve años.
She's nine.

Ella va a una escuela primaria.
She goes to grammar (primary) school.

D. PROFESSIONS

¿En qué trabaja?
What do you do?

Soy abogado.
I'm a lawyer.

¿Dónde trabaja?
Where do you work?

¿Cuál es su profesión?
What's your profession?

¿Qué hace su esposa?
What does your wife do?

¿Qué hace su marido?
What does your husband do?

¿Qué hace su madre?
What does your mother do?

¿Qué hace su padre?
What does your father do?

Es abogado.
He's a lawyer.

Es arquitecto.
He's an architect.

Es maestro.
He's a teacher.

Es maestra.
She's a teacher.

Es profesor de la Universidad.
He's a university professor.

Es médico.
He's a doctor.

Es comerciante.
He's a businessman.

Es mujer de negocios.
She's a businesswoman.

Es hombre de negocios.
He's a businessman.

Es agricultor.
He's a farmer.

Es funcionario público.
He's in the government service.

Trabaja en una fábrica de automóviles.
He works in an automobile factory.

Trabaja de sol a sombra.
She works from morning till night.

E. Family Matters

¿Tiene usted parientes aquí?
Do you have any relatives here?

¿Vive aquí toda su familia?
Does all your family live here?

Toda mi familia menos mis abuelos.
All my family except my grandparents.

Ellos viven en una finca cerca de Toledo.
They live on a farm near Toledo.

¿Es usted pariente del señor Villanueva?
Are you related to Mr. Villanueva?

Es mi tío.
He's my uncle.

Es mi primo.
He's my cousin.

¿Es usted pariente de la señora García?
Are you related to Mrs. Garcia?

Es mi tía.
She's my aunt.

Es mi prima.
She's my cousin.

F. WORD STUDY

cómico	comedian, funny
contador	counter, accountant
detalle	detail
empleado	employee
juicio	judgment
músculo	muscle
parque	park
restaurante	restaurant
rosa	rose

LESSON 34

A. SHOPPING (*DE COMPRAS*)

1. **¿Cuánto es esto?**
   How much is this?

2. **Diez mil pesetas.**
   Ten thousand pesetas.

3. **Es bastante caro. ¿No tiene usted algo más barato?**
   That's rather expensive. Don't you have anything cheaper?

4. **¿En el mismo género?**
   Of the same sort?

5. **En el mismo género u otro parecido.**
   The same sort or something similar.

6. **Aquí tiene éste.**
   There's this.

7. **¿No tiene usted algo en otra clase que me pueda mostrar?**
   Haven't you any other kind you could show me?

8. **¿De menos precio?**
   Less expensive?

9. **Si es posible . . .**
   If ("it's") possible.

10. **Acaso sea éste el que usted quiere.**
    Perhaps you would like this?

11. **Depende del precio.**
    That depends on the price.

12. **Este vale ochocientas pesetas.**
    This one is eight hundred pesetas.

13. **Me gusta más que el otro.**
    I like it better than the other one.

14. **Es más barato.**
    It's cheaper.

15. **Y este otro, ¿es más barato o más caro?**
    How about this? Is it cheaper or more expensive?

16. **Es más caro.**
    It's more expensive.

17. **¿Y no tiene usted más surtido?**
    Haven't you anything else in stock?

18. **Estoy esperando recibir algunas novedades en breve.**
I'm hoping to receive some new styles soon.

19. **¿Para cuándo?**
How soon?

20. **De un día a otro. ¿Puede usted pasar por aquí a fines de semana?**
Any day now. Can you drop in towards the end of the week?

21. **Lo haré . . . ¿Y esto qué precio tiene?**
I'll do that. . . . What's the price of this?

22. **Quinientas pesetas, el par.**
Five hundred pesetas a pair.

23. **Déme usted una docena.**
Let me have a dozen.

24. **¿Se los lleva usted misma?**
Will you take them with you? ("Will you take them yourself?")

25. **Prefiero que me los envíe.**
I'd rather have you send them.

26. **¿A las mismas señas de siempre?**
Is the address still the same?

27. **Las mismas.**
The same.

28. **Buenos días.**
Good-bye.

29. Adiós.
Good-bye.

NOTES

1. [1]*Valer* to be worth, to amount to. *¿Qué vale esto?*
   ("What is this worth?[2]") How much is this? You
   can also say: *¿Cuánto vale? (¿Cuánto cuesta?)*
   How much is it? *¿Qué precio tiene? (¿Cuál es el
   precio?)* What's the price? *¿A cómo es eso?*
   What's the price of that? *¿A cuánto están las
   naranjas? (¿A cómo están las naranjas?) ¿A
   cómo vende usted las naranjas?* ("For how much
   do you sell the oranges?") How much are the
   oranges?

2. *Es bastante caro* That's rather expensive. *Muy
   caro* or *carísimo* very expensive (see p. 279).—
   Barato cheap. *Más barato* cheaper (see p. 279).
   Muy barato or *baratísimo* very cheap.

5. *Género* kind, class, sort.

6. "Here you have this."

7. "Haven't you anything in another kind you could
   show me?" *Muéstreme alguna otra cosa.* Show
   me something else. You can also say: *Enséñeme
   alguna otra cosa. Mostrar* and *enseñar* both
   mean "to show."

8. *De menos precio* "of less price."

10. *Sea* from *ser* (see p. 339).—"Perhaps this is
    what you want (would like)?"

11. *Depender de* to depend upon.

13. *Me gusta más* I like it more (see p. 150).

15. *Y este otro.* "And this other one."

17. *Surtido* assortment, supply, stock. "And haven't
    you more stock?"

---

[1] Numbers refer to the sentences above.
[2] Words in quotation marks are literal translations.

18. *Estoy esperando* I'm expecting (see p. 334). *Novedad* latest style, latest fashion. *Novedades* new styles. *La última novedad* the latest news; the latest styles. *¿Hay alguna novedad?* Is there anything new? *Sin novedad* as usual; nothing new. *No hay novedad.* There's nothing new.—*En breve* in brief; in a short time.

19. *¿Para cuándo?* "For when?"

20. *De un día a otro* "From one day to the next." *Pasar por aquí* to pass by here, to stop in here.

21. *Lo haré* I'll do that. *Haré* is from *hacer* to make, do (see p. 224).

23. *Déme.* Give me. *Dé* is from *dar* (see p. 227); *me* me. Notice that the *me* is written together with the *dé* (see p. 301).

25. *Prefiero que . . .* I'd prefer that . . . , I'd rather.

26. "The same address as always?" *Las mismas* the same. The form is feminine plural because it refers to *señas* (address) which is feminine plural. The word *domicilio* also means address. However, when using the same, it would remain singular and would be in the masculine form, *mismo,* to agree with *domicilio.*

28. *Hasta otro día* "Until another day." Other expressions: *Hasta mañana* "Until tomorrow." *Hasta la vista.* "Until we see one another again." *Hasta luego.* See you soon. *Nos vemos.* See you. ("We'll see each other.") *Adiós.* Goodbye. *Que lo pase usted bien. (Páselo usted bien.)* ("May you get along well.") Good-bye. *Quede usted con Dios (Queden ustedes con Dios).* "Remain with God" (said by person leaving). *Vaya usted con Dios (Vayan ustedes con Dios).* "Go with God" (said by person remaining behind). *Si Dios quiere.* God willing. (Said by either or both persons.)

QUIZ 31

1. *Es bastante* _____ (expensive).
   a. *vale*
   b. *esto*
   c. *caro*

2. *No tiene usted algo más* _____ (cheap).
   a. *género*
   b. *precio*
   c. *barato*

3. *En el* _____ (same) *género*.
   a. *algo*
   b. *mismo*
   c. *más*

4. *De* _____ (less) *precio*.
   a. *más*
   b. *menos*
   c. *mismo*

5. *Me gusta éste* _____ (more) *que el otro*.
   a. *acaso*
   b. *más*
   c. *vale*

6. *¿No* _____ (have) *usted más surtido?*
   a. *tiene*
   b. *caro*
   c. *otro*

7. *Estoy esperando* _____ (receive) *novedades*.
   a. *preferencia*
   b. *tranquilo*
   c. *recibir*

8. ¿Para _____ (when)?
   a. *surtido*
   b. *caro*
   c. *cuándo*

9. *A las mismas* _____ (address) *de siempre?*
   a. *señas*
   b. *domicilio*
   c. *envíe*

ANSWERS
1—c; 2—c; 3—b; 4—b; 5—b; 6—a; 7—c; 8—c;
9—a.

B. GENERAL SHOPPING EXPRESSIONS

Quiero comprar . . .	I'd like to buy . . .
¿Cuánto cuesta?	How much is it?
¡Es muy caro!	It's very expensive!
¿Tiene uno más barato?	Do you have something cheaper?
Prefiero algo . . .	I prefer something . . .
Mi talla es . . .	My size is . . .
Me lo llevo.	I'll take it.

LESSON 35

A. BREAKFAST IN A RESTAURANT (*DESAYUNO EN UN RESTAURANTE*)

1. P[1]: ¿Tendrás apetito?
   P: You must be hungry. ("You're probably hungry.")

[1] *P* stands here for *Pedro* "Peter"; *J* for *Juan* "John"; *L* for *Luisa* "Louise"; *M* for *Mozo* "Waiter."

2. **J: Sí que lo tengo.**
   J: I certainly am. ("I certainly have.")

3. **L: Yo tengo una hambre canina.**
   L: I'm terribly hungry.

4. **P: ¡Camarero! ¡Camarero!**
   P: Waiter! Waiter!

5. **M: Díganme, señores.**
   M: Yes, folks.

6. **P: Queremos desayuno para tres personas.**
   P: We'd like breakfast for three.

7. **L: ¿Qué podría servirnos?**
   L: What can you serve us?

8. **M: Café con leche, té con limón o con leche, chocolate . . .**
   M: Coffee with milk, tea with lemon or with milk, chocolate . . .

9. **P: ¿Con qué lo sirven?**
   P: What do you serve with it?

10. **M: Con panecillos, bizcochos. . . .**
    M: Rolls, biscuits . . .

11. **L: ¿Hay mantequilla?**
    L: Is there any butter?

12. **M: Sí, señora.**
    M: Yes, Madame.

13. **J: Tráigame una taza de café con leche y panecillos.**
    J: Bring me a cup of coffee and some rolls.

14. **P: Tráigame a mí lo mismo.**
    P: Bring me the same.

15. **J: Y usted, Luisa. ¿Qué va a comer?**
    J: And you, Louise? What are you going to eat?

16. **L: Yo como muy poco.**
    L: I don't eat very much.

17. **J: La línea. ¿No es así?**
    J: Your figure, I suppose?

18. **L: No precisamente ... más que nada es mi costumbre.**
    L: Not exactly—habit more than anything else.

19. **M: Usted me dirá, señora.**
    M: What will you have, Madame?

20. **L: Té con limón, galletas y un huevo.**
    L: Tea and lemon, biscuits, and an egg.

21. **J: Mozo, ¿quiere usted traerme una servilleta?**
    J: Waiter, would you please bring me a napkin?

22. **L: Y a mí me trae un tenedor, por favor.**
    L: And a fork for me, please.

23. **J: Haga el favor de traernos un poco más de azúcar.**
    P: Please bring us a little more sugar.

24. **P: Y después nos dará la cuenta ... Ahí tiene, camarero.**
    J: And then let's have the check. ... Here you are, waiter.

25. M: Muchas gracias, señor.
   M: Thank you, sir.

NOTES

1. *Tendrás, lit.*, "you will have." This is the future familiar singular form used with people you know well. The future is used to express the concept of probability in the present.
2. "Yes, I have."
3. *Tengo una hambre canina.* I'm hungry as a wolf ("as a dog"). *Canino* canine. The common word for "dog" is *perro. Tengo* (I have) is from *tener* to have (see p. 227).
4. *Camarero* waiter (*camarera* waitress). Another word used often in Spain for "waiter" is *mozo (moza),* while *mesero (mesera)* is used in Mexico. *Señor, Señora,* and *Señorita* may also be used.
5. *Díganme señores.* "Tell me, ladies and gentlemen" (ma'am and sir). *Digan* (they say) is from *decir* to say (see p. 228).
6. *Queremos* we would like; from *querer* to want, like (see p. 228).
7. *Podría* could you; from *poder* to be able (see p. 232). *Servirnos* to serve us. Notice that the *nos* ("us") is added directly to *servir* (see p. 301).
9. *¿Con qué lo sirven?* What do you serve with it? *Desayuno* is a light breakfast consisting usually of coffee and rolls, or else chocolate with biscuits or coffee cake. The regular restaurants don't usually serve breakfast; only hotels and cafés do.
10. *Panecillos* rolls. *Bollo* is also common for roll. In some Spanish-speaking countries, *bizcocho* is sponge cake.
16. "I eat very little."

17. "Your figure, isn't it?" *Línea* line; here it means "figure." *Guardar la línea* to keep one's figure.
18. "More than anything else it's my habit. *Costumbre* habit; custom.
19. *Decir* to say. *Usted me dirá, señorita* ("You will say.") What will you have, Miss? Other uses of *Usted dirá: Sírvame un poco de coñac.—Usted dirá.* May I have a little brandy.—Say when. *Tengo algo que decirle—Usted dirá.* I have something to tell you.—Go ahead. *¿Le prestamos el dinero?—Usted dirá.* Shall we lend him the money?—It's up to you to say. You decide.
20. *Huevo* egg. *Un par de huevos fritos* two fried eggs. *Huevos pasados por agua* soft-boiled eggs. *Huevos revueltos* scrambled eggs.
22. "And to me bring a fork."
23. "Do the favor of bringing us a little more (of) sugar."
24. "And then you will give us the check." *Dará* you will give; from *dar* to give (see p. 227). *Quedar* to remain, stay. *Se quedó en casa.* He stayed at home. *Quedar* is often used where we use the verb "to be": *¿Dónde queda el hotel?* Where is the hotel? *Quedarse con algo* to keep something.—Another word for "change" is *cambio*.

QUIZ 32

1. _____ (We want) *desayuno para tres personas.*
   a. *Queremos*
   b. *Desayunar*
   c. *Apetito*

2. ¿_____ (Is there) *mantequilla?*
    a. *Sirven*
    b. *Hay*
    c. *Podría*

3. *Tráigame a mí lo* _____ (same)
    a. *muy*
    b. *mismo*
    c. *espere*

4. ¿*Qué va a* _____ (eat)?
    a. *sirven*
    b. *poco*
    c. *comer*

5. *Yo como muy* _____ (little).
    a. *va*
    b. *esto*
    c. *poco*

6. *Quiere usted* _____ (bring me) *una servilleta.*
    a. *costumbre*
    b. *traerme*
    c. *dirá*

7. _____ (Afterwards) *nos dará la cuenta.*
    a. *Favor*
    b. *Tenedor*
    c. *Después*

ANSWERS
1—a; 2—b; 3—b; 4—c; 5—c; 6—b; 7—c.

B. To Eat: *Comer*, to Drink: *Beber*, to Take: *Tomar*

1. To eat: *Comer*

yo como	*nosotros comemos*
tú comes	*vosotros coméis*
él come	*ellos comen*

No como carne.	I don't eat meat.
¡Come lo que sea!	He eats anything.
Comen con ganas.	They eat heartily.

2. To drink: *Beber*

yo bebo	*nosotros bebemos*
tú bebes	*vosotros bebéis*
él bebe	*ellos beben*

¿Quieres beber algo?	Do you want to drink something?
Bebe como una cuba.	He drinks like a fish.

3. To take: *Tomar*

yo tomo	*nosotros tomamos*
tú tomas	*vosotros tomáis*
él toma	*ellos toman*

Tomamos un bocadillo.	We're having a snack.
¿Qué toma?	What will you have to drink?
¿Puedo tomar su pedido?	Can I take your order?

C. A Sample Menu

MENU[1]	MENU
Entremeses variados	Hors d'oeuvres
Sopa de fideos	Noodle soup
Puré de guisantes	Pea soup
Tortilla de cebolla	Onion omelet
Arroz con pollo	Chicken and rice
Pollo asado	Roast chicken
Cordero asado	Roast lamb
Bistec con patatas fritas	Steak with French-fried potatoes
Ensalada de lechuga con tomate	Lettuce and tomato salad
Queso y fruta	Cheese and fruit
Café	Coffee

LESSON 36

A. Apartment Hunting (*A La Busca De Departamento*)

1. **Vengo a ver el departamento.**
   I've come to see ("I come to see") the apartment.

2. **¿Cuál de ellos?**
   Which one?

3. **El que está por alquilar.**
   The one that is for rent.

---

[1] Or, *(la) carta.*

4. **Hay dos.**
   There are two.

5. **¿Puede usted darme algún detalle de los departamentos?**
   Can you describe them?

6. **El del quinto piso es sin muebles.**
   The one on the fifth floor is unfurnished.

7. **¿Y el otro?**
   And the other one?

8. **El del segundo piso es amueblado.**
   The one on the second floor is furnished.

9. **¿Cuántas habitaciones tienen?**
   How many rooms do they have?

10. **El del quinto tiene cuatro habitaciones, cocina y baño.**
    The one on the fifth floor has four bedrooms, a kitchen and a bath.

11. **¿Da a la calle?**
    Does it face the street?

12. **No, da al patio.**
    No, it faces a courtyard.

13. **¿Cómo es el del segundo piso?**
    And the one on the second floor?

14. **El del segundo tiene un dormitorio, sala y comedor.**
    The one on the second floor has a bedroom, a living room, and a dining room.

15. **¿Da también al patio?**
Does it also face out on a courtyard?

16. **No, da a la calle.**
No, it faces the street.

17. **¿Cuánto es el alquiler?**
How much is the rent?

18. **El alquiler del más grande es quinientas mil pesetas al año, además del agua y el gas.**
The larger one is five hundred thousand pesetas a year, plus water and gas.

19. **¿Y el amueblado?**
And the furnished one?

20. **Éste cuesta un millón de pesetas al año, todo incluido.**
That one costs one million pesetas a year, everything included.

21. **¿Qué clase de muebles tiene? ¿Están los muebles en buen estado?**
What kind of furniture does it have? Is the furniture in good condition?

22. **Los muebles son modernos y están en magníficas condiciones.**
It's modern furniture and it's in excellent condition.

23. **Usted hallará todo lo que necesite, incluso un juego de utensilios de cocina.**
You'll find everything you need, even a complete set of kitchen utensils.

24. **¿Hay que firmar un contrato?**
Does one have to sign a lease?

25. **Para eso usted tendrá que ver al administrador.**
You'll have to see the renting agent for that.

26. **¿Cuáles son las condiciones?**
What are the terms?

27. **Un mes adelantado y otro de fianza.**
One month's rent in advance and another month's rent as a deposit.

28. **¿Es eso todo?**
Is that all?

29. **Por supuesto, usted tendrá que dar referencias.**
Of course, you'll have to give references.

30. **A propósito, ¿hay ascensor?**
By the way, is there an elevator?

31. **No, no hay ascensor.**
No, there isn't any elevator.

32. **¡Qué lástima!**
What a shame!

33. **Aparte de esto la casa es muy moderna.**
Aside from that, the house is very modern.

34. **¿Qué quiere usted decir?**
What do you mean?

35. **Hay calefacción y aire acondicionado central y escalera de servicio.**
There's central heating and air conditioning and a back stairway.

36. **Ah, se me olvidaba . . . ¿Hay agua caliente?**
Oh, I forgot. . . . Is there any hot water?

37. **¡Por supuesto! Los cuartos de baño han sido reformados recientemente.**
Of course! And the bathrooms were recently remodeled.

38. **¿Se pueden ver los departamentos?**
Can one see the apartments?

39. **Únicamente por la mañana.**
Only in the morning.

40. **Muy bien. Vendré mañana por la mañana. Muchas gracias.**
Very well, I'll come tomorrow morning. Thanks a lot.

41. **De nada.**
Not at all.

NOTES

1. The word *piso,* which is here used to mean "floor, building storey" is commonly used in Spain for *departamento.* In addition to *departamento,* the word *apartamento* is also widely used in Latin America and in the Spanish of the United States.
2. "Which of them?"

3. *Alquilar* to let, to lease, to rent, to hire.

5. "Can you give me some details about the apartments?"

6. *Sin muebles* ("without furniture") unfurnished. You can also say *No amueblado* or *sin amueblar*. *Muebles* furniture. *Amueblar* to furnish.

8. *Principal* (main, principal) is the first floor in Spain. *Los cuartos del principal* the apartments on the first floor. *Piso bajo* or *planta baja* ground floor. *El primer piso* (the first floor) in Spain usually corresponds to the second or third floor in the United States. In Latin America, however, floors are generally counted the way they are in the United States; for example, *el primer piso* in Mexico City corresponds to our "first floor."

9. Other words for "room" are *cuarto* and *pieza*.

11. *Da a la calle*. It faces the street. It overlooks the street. *Da* is from *dar* to give (see p. 227).

14. *Dormitorio* bedroom. You can also say *alcoba* and *cuarto de dormir*. *Comedor* dining room. *Baño* bath. *Cuarto de baño* bathroom. *cocina* kitchen.

20. *Cuesta* costs; from *costar* to cost (see p. 315).

21. Notice that the word for "furniture" *(los muebles)* is plural. *Estado* state, condition.

23. *Hallará* you will find. For the future tense (see p. 288).

24. *Contrato* contract, agreement, lease. *Contrato de arrendamiento* or *contrato* lease.

26. *¿Cuáles?* is the plural of *¿cuál?* what, which. It is plural here because it modifies *las condiciones,* which is plural.

27. *Un mes adelantado y otro de fianza* one month in advance and one month's deposit. *Adelantado* or *por adelantado* in advance. *Fianza* guarantee,

bond, security, bail. It's customary to leave a month's rent as a deposit and to pay a month's rent in advance.

34. *¿Qué quiere usted decir?* What do you mean?
36. *Se me olvidaba.* I forgot.
37. *Reformados* (remodeled) is masculine plural because it refers to *los cuartos.*

QUIZ 33

1. _____ (I come) *a ver el departamento.*
   a. *Viene*
   b. *Vengo*
   c. *Esta*

2. *El que* _____ (is) *de alquiler.*
   a. *ver*
   b. *ellos*
   c. *está*

3. _____ (There are) *dos.*
   a. *Hay*
   b. *Vengo*
   c. *Es*

4. *Es* _____ (without) *muebles.*
   a. *quinto*
   b. *otro*
   c. *sin*

5. *¿* _____ (How) *están dispuestas las habitaciones?*
   a. *Cuánto*
   b. *Cómo*
   c. *De*

6. ¿*Da a la* _____ (street)?
   a. *patio*
   b. *sala*
   c. *calle*

7. *Da* _____ (also) *al patio*.
   a. *también*
   b. *otro*
   c. *calle*

8. *Éste* _____ (costs) *un millón de australes*.
   a. *cuesta*
   b. *todo*
   c. *cuanto*

9. *Usted* _____ (will find) *todo*.
   a. *necesite*
   b. *firmar*
   c. *hallará*

10. *La casa es* _____ (very) *moderna*.
    a. *esto*
    b. *muy*
    c. *que*

ANSWERS
1—b; 2—c; 3—a; 4—c; 5—b; 6—c; 7—a; 8—a;
9—c; 10—b.

B. To Have: *TENER*

1. I have

tengo	*tenemos*
tienes	*tenéis*
tiene	*tienen*

Tengo esto.	I have this. I've got this.
No tengo nada.	I don't have anything.
¿Lo tiene usted?	Do you have it?
No lo tengo.	I don't have it.
Tengo tiempo.	I have time.
No tengo dinero.	I haven't any money.
No tengo tiempo.	I haven't any time.
No tiene amigos.	He hasn't any friends.
Tengo hambre.	I'm hungry.
Tengo sed.	I'm thirsty.
Tengo sueño.	I'm sleepy.
Tengo frió.	I'm cold.
Tengo calor.	I'm warm.
Tengo razón.	I'm right.
No tiene razón.	He's not right.
No tienen razón.	They're wrong.
¿Tiene usted amigos en Madrid?	Do you have (any) friends in Madrid?
No tengo amigos en Madrid.	I don't have any friends in Madrid.
¿Tiene usted un cigarrillo?	Do you have a cigarette?
No tengo cigarrillos.	I don't have any cigarettes.
¿Tiene usted fuego?	Do you have a light?
No tengo cerillos.	I don't have matches.
Tengo veinte años.	I'm twenty.
Tengo dolor de cabeza.	I have a headache.
Tengo dolor de muelas.	I have a toothache.
¿Qué tiene usted?	What's the matter with you?
No tengo nada.	Nothing's the matter with me.
¿Cuánto dinero tiene usted?	How much money do you have?

No tengo nada de dinero.	I haven't any money at all.
Tengo necesidad de ...	I need ...
Tengo necesidad de eso.	I need that.

2. *Tener que* translates "to have to":

Tengo que ir.	I have to go. I must go.
Tengo que irme.	I have to leave.
Tengo que escribir una carta.	I have to write a letter.
Tengo mucho que hacer.	I have a lot to do.

3. Do I Have It?

¿Lo tengo yo?	Do I have it?
¿Lo tienes tú?	Do you have it?
¿Lo tiene él?	Does he have it?
¿Lo tiene ella?	Does she have it?
¿Lo tenemos nosotros?	Do we have it?
¿Lo tenéis vosotros?	Do you have it?
¿Lo tienen ellos?	Do they have it?

4. Don't I Have It?

¿No lo tengo yo?	Don't I have it?
¿No lo tienes tú?	Don't you have it?
¿No lo tiene él?	Doesn't he have it?
¿No lo tiene ella?	Doesn't she have it?
¿No lo tenemos nosotros?	Don't we have it?
¿No lo tenéis vosotros?	Don't you have it?
¿No lo tienen ellos?	Don't they have it?

QUIZ 34

1. *No tengo dinero.*	a. I have a headache.
2. *No tengo nada.*	b. Don't you have it?
3. *No tiene razón.*	c. I don't have it.
4. *Tengo sueño.*	d. I'm cold.
5. *¿Lo tiene él?*	e. I'm warm.
6. *No lo tengo.*	f. I don't have any money.
7. *Tengo hambre.*	g. Does he have it?
8. *Tengo frío.*	h. He's not right.
9. *Tengo veinte años.*	i. I'm thirsty.
10. *¿No lo tienes tú?*	j. I have a lot to do.
11. *Tengo que irme.*	k. I don't have anything.
12. *Tengo calor.*	l. I'm sleepy.
13. *Tengo sed.*	m. I'm hungry.
14. *Tengo dolor de cabeza.*	n. I have to leave.
15. *Tengo mucho que hacer.*	o. I'm twenty years old.

ANSWERS

1—f; 2—k; 3—h; 4—l; 5—g; 6—c; 7—m; 8—d; 9—o; 10—b; 11—n; 12—e; 13—i; 14—a; 15—j.

C. To Have (Auxiliary): *Haber*

he	*hemos*
has	*habéis*
ha	*han*

1. *Haber* never means "to have" in the sense of "to possess" (*tener* is used in this sense). It is used with the past participle to form compound tenses:

He aprendido el español en México.	I have learned Spanish in Mexico.
He pasado una semana en Cuba.	I have spent a week in Cuba.
¿Has escrito la carta?	Have you written the letter?
¿Ha venido su hermano?	Has your brother come?

2. The third person singular *hay* means "there is" or "there are":

Hay mucha gente aquí.	There are a lot of people here.

Hubo and *Había* (see p. 335) mean "there was" or "there were":

Hubo un incendio.	There was a fire.
Había una casa allí.	There was a house there (there used to be a house there).

Habrá (see p. 335) means "there will be":

Habrá mucha gente.	There will be many people.
Habrá muchas casas allí.	There will be many houses there.

3. *Haber* is used some in expressions of weather:

Hay niebla.	It's foggy.
Hay humedad.	It's humid.

4. *Haber de* means "to have to":

Ha de hacerlo.	He has to do it.
He de ir al centro.	I have to go downtown.
Ha de venir mañana.	She has to come tomorrow.

5. *Hay que* means "it is necessary," "one has to," "one must":

Hay que aprender los verbos.	One must ("it is necessary to") learn the verbs.
Hay que dar vuelta a la derecha.	It's necessary to (you must, one must) turn ("given a turn") to the right.

D. To Do, To Make: *HACER*

hago	*hacemos*
haces	*hacéis*
hace	*hacen*

¿Cuánto tiempo le tomará para hacer esto?	How long will it take you to make (do) that?
¿Cómo se hace esto?	How do you make (do) this?
¿Qué haces?	What are you making (doing)?

| ¿Me puede enseñar cómo hacer esto? | Can you show me how to do this? |

1. The third person singular of *hacer* is used in expressions about the weather:

Hace (muy) buen tiempo.	The weather's nice. ("It's good weather.")
Hace (muy) mal tiempo.	The weather's bad. ("It's bad weather.")
Hace (mucho) frío.	It's (very) cold.
Hacía (mucho) calor.	It was (very) warm (hot).
Ha hecho (mucho) sol.	It's been (very) sunny.

2. *Hace* often translates "ago":

Hace tres años.	Three years ago.
Hace seis meses.	Six months ago.
Se lo dije hace tres semanas.	I told it to him three weeks ago.

3. Notice the use of *hacer* in these expressions of time:

| *Hace dos horas que estudio.* | I have been studying for two hours. ("It makes two hours that I study.") |
| *Hace un año que está en Madrid.* | He has been in Madrid for a year. ("It makes a year that he is in Madrid.") |

QUIZ 35

1. *Ha hecho sol.*	a. Six months ago.
2. *¿Qué haces?*	b. It's very cold.
3. *Hace buen tiempo.*	c. Three years ago.
4. *Hace dos horas que estudio.*	d. I told it to him three weeks ago.
5. *Hace un año que está en Madrid.*	e. What are you doing?
6. *Hace mucho frío.*	f. He has been in Madrid for a year.
7. *Hace tres años.*	g. It's been sunny.
8. *Se lo dije hace tres semanas.*	h. The weather is nice.
9. *¿Cómo se hace esto?*	i. I have been studying for two hours.
10. *Hace seis meses.*	j. How do you do this?

ANSWERS
1—g; 2—e; 3—h; 4—i; 5—f; 6—b; 7—c; 8—d; 9—j; 10—a.

LESSON 37

A. Could You Give Me Some Information?

1. Perdone usted.
Pardon me.

2. **¿En qué puedo servirle?**
   What can I do for you?

3. **¿Podría darme usted alguna información?**
   Could you give me some information?

4. **Con mucho gusto.**
   Gladly. ("With much pleasure.")

5. **No conozco la ciudad y no puedo orientarme.**
   I don't know this town and I can't find my way
   around.

6. **Pues, es muy sencillo.**
   Well, it's quite simple.

7. **Es que soy extranjero.**
   You see, I'm a stranger here.

8. **En ese caso le enseñaré la ciudad.**
   In that case, I'll show you the town.

9. **Pues, se lo agradecería mucho.**
   I'd appreciate that a lot. ("Then, I'd be very
   grateful to you.")

10. **¿Ve ese edificio grande de la esquina?**
    Do you see that large building on the corner?

11. **¿Aquél de la bandera?**
    The one with the flag?

12. **Exactamente. Ese es el Correo. Frente a él, al
    otro lado de la calle . . .**
    That's right. ("Exactly.") That's the Post Office.
    Opposite it, on the other side of the street . . .

13. **¿Dónde?**
    Where?

14. Allá. ¿Ve usted ese otro edificio con el reloj?
Over there. Do you see that other building with the clock?

15. Ah sí, ya veo.
Oh, yes, now I see.

16. Es el Ayuntamiento.
That's the City Hall.

17. Ya veo . . . A propósito, ¿cómo se llama esta calle?
Now I see. . . . By the way, what's the name of this street?

18. La calle Mayor.
Main Street.

19. ¿Dónde está la Comisaría de Policía?
Where is the police station?

20. Al final de la calle. Siga usted todo derecho.
At the end of the street. Go straight ahead.

21. ¿Y si la paso de largo?
What if I miss it?

22. No tiene pérdida. Es un edificio grande, rodeado de una verja . . . ¿Ve usted esa tienda?
You can't miss it. It's a big building surrounded by an iron fence . . . You see that store?

23. ¿Qué tienda? ¿La que está a la derecha?
Which store? The one on the right?

24. Exacto. Aquélla que tiene una cruz roja en el escaparate.
Right, the one with a large red cross in the window.

25. ¿Es una farmacia?
Is it a pharmacy?

26. Sí, es una farmacia. En la casa de al lado hay un médico. Su nombre está en la puerta.
Yes, it's a pharmacy. The doctor lives right next door. ("In the house to the side there is a doctor.") His name's on the door.

27. ¿Tiene la clínica en la misma casa en que vive?
Does he have his office there as well? ("Does he have his office in the same house in which he lives?")

28. Sí, pero se pasa las mañanas en el hospital.
Yes, but he spends every morning at the hospital.

29. ¿Dónde está el hospital?
Where's the hospital?

30. El hospital está a dos cuadras de aquí, un poco antes de llegar a la carretera.
The hospital is two blocks from here, just before ("a little before") you come to the main highway.

31. ¿Cómo puedo volver a mi hotel?
How can I get back to my hotel?

32. Vaya usted por aquí. Lo ve allí, junto al . . .
Go this way. You see it there, next to the . . .

33. . . . cine. ¿No es así?
. . . movies. That's right, isn't it? ("isn't it so?").

34. Exacto.
Yes. ("Exact.")

35. **Ya me doy cuenta.**
Now I understand.

36. **¿Por qué no se compra usted una guía?**
Why don't you buy yourself a guidebook?

37. **No es mala idea. ¿Dónde podría comprar una?**
That's not a bad idea. Where can I buy one?

38. **En la estación o en cualquier kiosco de periódicos.**
In the station or at any newspaper stand.

39. **¿Está lejos la estación de aquí?**
Is the station far from here?

40. **La estación está al final del Paseo de las
Delicias.**
The station is at the end of Delicias Avenue.

41. **¿Dónde hay un kiosco de periódicos por aquí?**
Where's there a newspaper stand near here?

42. **En la esquina tiene usted uno.**
There's one on this corner. ("On the corner you
have one.")

43. **Le estoy muy agradecido.**
Thank you very much. ("I'm very grateful to
you.")

44. **No tiene importancia. Me ha sido muy grato
haberle sido útil.**
Not at all. ("It has no importance.") I'm very
glad to have been of any help to you. ("I've been
very glad to have been useful to you.")

45. He tenido una gran suerte en haberlo encontrado. Verdaderamente usted conoce muy bien la ciudad.
I was certainly lucky to meet you. You really know this town very well.

46. No es para menos. ¡Soy el alcalde!
It's not surprising. I'm the mayor!

NOTES

1. *Perdone usted.* Pardon me. I beg your pardon. *Dispense usted.* Excuse me. *Hágame el favor* . . . ("Do me the favor . . .") Please . . . *Me hace el favor* . . . ("Do me the favor . . .") Will you please . . . *¿Me hace el favor de decirme?* Will you please tell me? *Tenga la bondad* ("Have the goodness to . . .") Please . . . *Sírvase decirme.* Please tell me. *¿Puede decirme?* Can you tell me? *Le agradecería que* . . . I'd appreciate it if . . . *or* I'd be obliged to you if . . .

2. *Puedo.* I can; from *poder* to be able (see p. 232).

3. *¿Podría usted?* Could you?; from *poder* (see p. 232).

5. *Conozco.* I know; from *conocer* to know (see p. 326). *Orientarse* to orient oneself, to get one's bearings, to find one's way.

7. "It's that I'm a stranger." *Es que* the reason is that . . . *or* It's because . . .

8. *Enseñar* to show, to teach.

9. *Se lo agradecería.* I would be grateful (see p. 291).

11. *Bandera* flag. Every public building in Spain and Latin America has a flag flying above the main entrance.

12. *Correo* mail. *El correo* the post office. *¿Dónde está el correo?* Where's the post office? Also *la casa de correos* and *la oficina de correos*. *¿A qué hora reparten el correo?* When is the mail distributed? At what time do they distribute the mail?

21. *Pasar de largo* to pass by without stopping, to pass by without noticing a place; to miss a place.

22. *Pérdida* loss. *No tiene pérdida*. ("It has no loss.") You can't miss it.

27. *Tiene* he has; from *tener* to have (see p. 227). *Clínica* clinic; doctor's office. A "doctor's office" is also called *consultorio*.

30. *El hospital está a dos cuadras de aquí*. This is the expression used in Latin America. In Spain you might say *El hospital está pasadas dos bocacalles*. ("The hospital is two street intersections passed.")

31. *Volver* to return.

35. *Doy* I give; from *dar* to give (see p. 227). *Cuenta* account; bill, check.

44. *Ha sido*. It has been; from *ser* (see p. 335).

45. *He tenido* I have had; from *tener*.

46. *No es para menos*. ("It's not for less."). It's no wonder. It's not surprising.—*Soy* I am; from *ser* (see p. 339).

QUIZ 36

1. *Es muy _____* (simple).
   a. *pues*
   b. *sencillo*
   c. *ciudad*

2. *Le enseñaré la* _____ (city).
   a. *caso*
   b. *ciudad*
   c. *orientar*

3. *Ese edificio grande de la* _____ (corner).
   a. *esquina*
   b. *calle*
   c. *correo*

4. *Pues ése es el* _____ (post office).
   a. *calle*
   b. *correo*
   c. *otro*

5. *¿Ve usted esa* _____ (store)?
   a. *derecha*
   b. *tienda*
   c. *casa*

6. *En la casa de al lado hay un* _____ (doctor).
   a. *médico*
   b. *farmacia*
   c. *nombre*

7. *Su nombre está en la* _____ (door).
   a. *misma*
   b. *puerta*
   c. *clínica*

8. *Tiene la clínica en la misma* _____ (house) *en que vive.*
   a. *puerta*
   b. *lado*
   c. *casa*

9. *Un poco* _____ (before) *de llegar a la carre-tera.*
   a. *después*
   b. *antes*
   c. *pasadas*

10. *¿Dónde podría* _____ (buy) *una?*
    a. *comprar*
    b. *guía*
    c. *estación*

ANSWERS
1—b; 2—b; 3—a; 4—b; 5—b; 6—a; 7—b; 8—c;
9—b; 10—a.

B. SIGHT-SEEING

¿Cuáles son los sitios históricos?
Which are the historic sights?

¿Dónde hay una tienda de recuerdos?
Where is a souvenir shop?

Quiero ir al sector comercial.
I want to go to the business district.

Quiero ir al palacio de gobierno.
I want to go to the government palace.

La vista es impresionante.
The view is breathtaking.

Este lugar es muy turístico.
This place is very touristy.

LESSON 38

A. THE MEDIA AND COMMUNICATIONS
(*LOS MEDIOS DE COMUNICACIÓN*)

1. **Hugo: No quería que compraras el peródico de hoy.**
Hugo: I didn't want you to buy the newspaper today.

2. **Gabriela: ¿Por qué? ¿Qué hubo?**
Gabriela: Why not? What Happened?

3. **H: Los titulares de los periódicos traen noticias chocantes. La primera plana presenta noticias de desastres, robos, asesinatos, violaciones, guerras, y sequias—nada mas.**
H: The newspaper headlines bring shocking news. The front page has news about disasters, robberies, murders, rapes, wars, and droughts—nothing else.

4. **G: Sería mejor que no hubiera tales noticias, pero ellas representan hechos reales.**
G: It would be better if there weren't any such news, but they are real events.

5. **H: ¡Ojalá que aprendiéramos del pasado!**
H: If only we learned from the past.

6. **G: Tal vez no debieras leer la primer plana ni los editoriales, para evitar las noticias chocantes.**
G: Maybe you shouldn't read the first page or the editorials in order to avoid the shocking news.

**7. H: Poco me interesan las secciones de finan-
zas, deportes, reseñas de libros o clasificados.**
H: The financial pages, sports, book reviews,
and classified sections don't interest me much.

**8. G: Podrías entretenerte con el crucigrama y
las tiras cómicas o los chismes.**
G: You could entertain yourself with the cross-
word puzzle and the comic strips or the gossip
column.

9. H: Es mejor no comprar el periódico, no leerlo.
H: It's better not to buy the paper, . . . not to
read it.

**10. G: La culpa no la tiene sólo la prensa. Los
satélites y el fax permiten que hoy día sepa-
mos todas las desgarcias mundiales con
mayor rapidez. Pero siempre hay algo intere-
sante, ¡y estoy segura que habrá buenas noticias tambien!**
G: It's not only the fault of the press. Satellites
and fax machines allow us to learn all the
world's misfortunes with greater speed. But
there's always something interesting, and I'm
sure that there will be good news, too!

B. AT THE AIRPORT
(EN EL AEROPUERTO)

**1. Francisca: Con permiso, señor, aquí tiene
nuestros pasajes, pasaportes y visas.**
Francisca: Pardon me, sir, here are our tickets,
passports and visas.

2. **Enrique: Perdóneme, señora. Este pasaporte no es suyo. Es de una niña.**
   Enrique: Excuse me, madam. This passport isn't yours. It belongs to a young girl.

3. **F: ¿No es mío? ¡Caray! Disculpe; sí que me he equivocado. La hija nuestra no viaja con nosotros. Momentito. Pues . . . es éste mio.**
   F: It isn't mine? Damn! I'm sorry; I have indeed made a mistake. Our daughter isn't traveling with us. One moment. Well this is the one.

4. **E: El vuelo está astrasado. Saldrá de la Puerta 23 a las ocho y media. ¿Desean Uds. facturar maletas?**
   E: The flight is delayed. It will leave from gate 23 at 8:30. Do you want to check luggage?

5. **F: La mía no, pero la suya sí.**
   F: Mine no, but his yes.

6. **E: Aquí está el recibo. Váyanse Uds. a la derecha. Pasen por la seguridad, y luego tendrán que hacer una declaración en la Aduana.**
   E: Here is the receipt. Go to the right. Pass through security and then you will have to make a Customs declaration.

7. **F: Queremos escoger asientos en la sección de no fumar.**
   F: We want to choose seats in the no-smoking section.

8. **E: En la puerta de embarque misma habrá un agente que les asignará asientos. ¡Buen viaje!**
   E: Right at the departure gate there'll be an agent who will assign you seats. Have a good trip!

QUIZ 37

A. LOS MEDIOS DE COMUNICACIÓN

1. ¿De qué están hablando?
   a. guerra
   b. el periódico
   c. la prensa

2. ¿De qué deberíamos de aprender?
   a. del futuro
   b. del presente
   c. del pasado

3. ¿Cómo llegan las noticias?
   a. por televisión
   b. por satélite
   c. por teléfono

4. La primera plana presenta _____ (news) chocantes.
   a. deportes
   b. hechos
   c. noticias

5. Un periódico tiene varias _____ (sections).
   a. desastres
   b. secciones
   c. titulares

B. EN EL AEROPUERTO

1. ¿De quién era el pasaporte?
   a. una niña
   b. la señora
   c. el hombre

2. ¿En dónde se quieren sentar?
   a. primera clase
   b. sección de fumar
   c. sección de no fumar

3. El vuelo está _____ (late).
   a. atrasado
   b. aquí
   c. temprano

4. Tenemos que pasar por la _____ (Customs).
   a. izquierda
   b. Aduana
   c. seguridad

5. Nuestra hija no ——— (travel) con nosotros.
   a. comé
   b. trabaja
   c. viaja

ANSWERS
A.
1—b; 2—c; 3—b; 4—c; 5—b;
B.
1—a; 2—c; 3—a; 4—b; 5—c.

C. THE MOST COMMON VERBS AND THEIR FORMS

1. To Do, To Make: *Hacer*

PRESENT	PAST	FUTURE	IMPERATIVE
hago	*hice*	*haré*	*haz (fam.)*
haces	*hiciste*	*harás*	*haga (pol.)*
hace	*hizo*	*hará*	*hagamos*

PRESENT	PAST	FUTURE	IMPERATIVE
hacemos	*hicimos*	*haremos*	*haced (fam.)*
hacéis	*hicisteis*	*haréis*	*hagan (pol.)*
hacen	*hicieron*	*harán*	

Lo hice yo mismo.	I made (did) it myself.
Harán siempre lo que se les mande.	They'll always do what they're told.
Haré lo posible por ir.	I'll do my best to go.
Hazlo lo más pronto posible.	Do it as soon as possible.

2. To Have (Auxiliary): *Haber*

PRESENT	PAST	FUTURE	IMPERATIVE
he	*hube*	*habré*	*he (fam.)*
has	*hubiste*	*habrás*	*haya (pol.)*
ha	*hubo*	*habrá*	*hayamos*
			habed (fam.)
hemos	*hubimos*	*habremos*	*hayan (pol.)*
habéis	*hubisteis*	*habréis*	
han	*hubieron*	*habrán*	

He tratado de comunicarme con él, pero ha sido imposible.	I tried to get in touch with him but it was impossible.

He aquí los libros que me prestaste.	Here are the books you lent me.
¿Has ido alguna vez a la ópera?	Have you ever been to the opera?
Han ido varias veces a su casa.	They've been to his house several times.
Habrá que ir mañana otra vez.	We'll have to go again tomorrow.

3. To Go: *Ir*

PRESENT	PAST	FUTURE	IMPERATIVE
voy	*fui*	*iré*	*ve (fam.)*
vas	*fuiste*	*irás*	*vaya (pol.)*
va	*fue*	*irá*	*vayamos id (fam.)*
vamos	*fuimos*	*iremos*	*vayan (pol.)*
vais	*fuisteis*	*iréis*	
van	*fueron*	*irán*	

Voy a ir a Sudamérica el año que viene.	I'm going to South America next year.
El va a ir sin usted.	He's going to go without you.
Fui a verlo ayer.	I went to see him yesterday.
Iré a visitarlas mañana.	I'll go to visit them tomorrow.
Vete pronto.	Go quickly.
¿Fuiste ayer al cine?	Did you go to the movies yesterday?
¡Vamos!	Let's go!
Anoche fuimos al teatro.	We went to the theater last night.

4. To Come: *Venir*

PRESENT	PAST	FUTURE	IMPERATIVE
vengo	*vine*	*vendré*	*ven (fam.)*
vienes	*viniste*	*vendrás*	*venga (pol.)*
viene	*vino*	*vendrá*	*vengamos*
			venid (fam.)
venimos	*vinimos*	*vendremos*	*vengan (pol.)*
venís	*vinisteis*	*vendréis*	
vienen	*vinieron*	*vendrán*	

Tú vienes conmigo, ¡verdad?	You're coming with me, aren't you?
El siempre viene a mi casa.	He always comes to my house.
¿Cuándo viene ella?	When will she come?
Ellos vienen a menudo a la ciudad.	They come to the city often.
Ellos vienen a vernos mañana.	They're coming to see us tomorrow.
Vendrán a vernos esta tarde.	They'll come to see us this afternoon.
Ven a esta misma hora mañana.	Come about this time tomorrow.

5. To Walk, To Go: *Andar*

PRESENT	PAST	FUTURE	IMPERATIVE
ando	*anduve*	*andaré*	*anda (fam.)*
andas	*anduviste*	*andarás*	*ande (pol.)*
anda	*anduvo*	*andará*	*andemos*
			andad (fam.)
andamos	*anduvimos*	*andaremos*	*anden (pol.)*
andáis	*anduvisteis*	*andaréis*	
andan	*anduvieron*	*andarán*	

Anduve a pie todo el camino.	I walked all the way.
Andaremos juntos.	We'll walk together.
Anda más de prisa.	Walk faster.

6. To Give: *Dar*

PRESENT	PAST	FUTURE	IMPERATIVE
doy	*di*	*daré*	*da (fam.)*
das	*diste*	*darás*	*dé (pol.)*
da	*dio*	*dará*	*demos*
			dad (fam.)
damos	*dimos*	*daremos*	*den (pol.)*
dais	*disteis*	*daréis*	
dan	*dieron*	*darán*	

¿Puede usted dármelo mañana?	Can you give it to me tomorrow?
Se lo di ayer.	I gave it to him yesterday.
Daré lo que pueda.	I'll give what I can.

7. To Have, To Hold: *Tener*

PRESENT	PAST	FUTURE	IMPERATIVE
tengo	*tuve*	*tendré*	*ten (fam.)*
tienes	*tuviste*	*tendrás*	*tenga (pol.)*
tiene	*tuvo*	*tendrá*	*tengamos*
			tened (fam.)
tenemos	*tuvimos*	*tendremos*	*tengan (pol.)*
tenéis	*tuvisteis*	*tendréis*	
tienen	*tuvieron*	*tendrán*	

No tengo tiempo.	I haven't any time.
Usted tiene que conseguirlo cuanto antes.	You have to get it as soon as possible.

Tenemos visitas en casa.	We have guests at home.
Tuvo que salir tem-prano hoy.	He had to go out early today.
¿Tendrá usted tiempo?	Will you have time?
Tengo que ir a un con-cierto esta noche.	I have to go to a concert tonight.

8. To Say: *Decir*

PRESENT	PAST	FUTURE	IMPERATIVE
digo	*dije*	*diré*	*di (fam.)*
dices	*dijiste*	*dirás*	*diga (pol.)*

PRESENT	PAST	FUTURE	IMPERATIVE
dice	*dijo*	*dirá*	*digamos*
			decid (fam.)
decimos	*dijimos*	*diremos*	*digan (pol.)*
decís	*dijisteis*	*diréis*	
dicen	*dijeron*	*dirán*	

El dijo que se iba.	He said he was leaving.
Ella dice que vendrá mañana.	She says she'll come to-morrow.
Ellos nunca dicen nada.	They never say any-thing.
Siempre dice lo que piensa.	He always says what he thinks.
Di lo que quieras.	Say whatever you like.
¿Qué piensa usted que dirá?	What do you think he'll say?

9. To Put: *Poner*

PRESENT	PAST	FUTURE	IMPERATIVE
pongo	*puse*	*pondré*	*pon (fam.)*
pones	*pusiste*	*pondrás*	*ponga (pol.)*
pone	*puso*	*pondrá*	*pongamos*
			poned (fam.)

ponemos	pusimos	pondremos	pongan (pol.)
ponéis	pusisteis	pondréis	
ponen	pusieron	pondrán	

Lo puse sobre la mesa.	I put it on the table.
¿Dónde lo vas a poner?	Where are you going to put it?
Pon las cosas en su lugar.	Put everything in its place.
Poned la mesa cerca de la ventana.	Put the table near the window.

10. To Put (On): *Ponerse*

PRESENT	PAST	FUTURE
me pongo	me puse	me pondré
te pones	te pusiste	te pondrás
se pone	se puso	se pondrá
nos ponemos	nos pusimos	nos pondremos
os ponéis	os pusisteis	os pondréis
se ponen	se pusieron	se pondrán.

Me puse tu sombrero por equivocación.	I put your hat on by mistake.
Ponte tu traje nuevo.	Put on your new suit.
Nos pusimos a jugar a las cartas.	We began to play cards.
El sol se pone a las cinco.	The sun sets at five.
Se pondrá furioso cuando lo sepa.	He'll be furious when he finds out.

11. To Wish, To Want: *Querer*

PRESENT	PAST	FUTURE	IMPERATIVE
quiero	quise	querré	quiere (fam.)
quieres	quisiste	querrás	quiera (pol.)

quiere	*quiso*	*querrá*	*queramos*
			quered (fam.)
queremos	*quisimos*	*querremos*	*quieran (pol.)*
queréis	*quisisteis*	*querréis*	
quieren	*quisieron*	*querrán*	

Quiero ir.	I want to go.
La quiso mucho	He loved her very much.
No querrá ir si no le acompañamos.	He won't want to go if we don't go with him.

12. To Bring: *Traer*

PRESENT	PAST	FUTURE	IMPERATIVE
traigo	*traje*	*traeré*	*trae (fam.)*
traes	*trajiste*	*traerás*	*traiga (pol.)*
trae	*trajo*	*traerá*	*traigamos*
			traed (fam.)
traemos	*trajimos*	*traeremos*	*traigan (pol.)*
traéis	*trajisteis*	*traeréis*	
traen	*trajeron*	*traerán*	

Se me olvidó traerlo.	I forgot to bring it.
Trae algún dinero contigo.	Bring some money with you.
Le trajo un regalo.	He brought her a present.

13. To Leave: *Salir*

PRESENT	PAST	FUTURE	IMPERATIVE
salgo	*salí*	*saldré*	*sal (fam.)*
sales	*saliste*	*saldrás*	*salga (pol.)*
sale	*salió*	*saldrá*	*salgamos*
			salid (fam.)
salimos	*salimos*	*saldremos*	*salgan*

salís	*salisteis*	*saldréis*
salen	*salieron*	*saldrán*

Salgo el miércoles. — I'm leaving on Wednesday.
Salió por aquí. — He went out this way.

14. To See: *Ver*

PRESENT	PAST	FUTURE	IMPERATIVE
veo	*vi*	*veré*	*ve (fam.)*
ves	*viste*	*verás*	*vea (pol.)*
ve	*vio*	*verá*	*veamos*
			ved (fam.)
vemos	*vimos*	*veremos*	*vean (pol.)*
veis	*visteis*	*veréis*	
ven	*vieron*	*verán*	

No ve bien sin sus anteojos. — He can't see well without his glasses.
Lo vi ayer. — I saw him yesterday.
Ya verás que lo que digo es verdad. — Now you'll see that what I say is true.

15. To Know: *Saber*

PRESENT	PAST	FUTURE	IMPERATIVE
sé	*supe*	*sabré*	*sabe (fam.)*
sabes	*supiste*	*sabrás*	*sepa (pol.)*
sabe	*supo*	*sabrá*	*sepamos*
			sabed (fam.)
sabemos	*supimos*	*sabremos*	*sepan (pol.)*
sabéis	*supisteis*	*sabréis*	
saben	*supieron*	*sabrán*	

Sé que eso es cierto. — I know it's true.
¿Supiste la noticia? — Did you hear the news?

Ya lo sabrán a tiempo.   They'll find it out in
                                                       time.

16. *Poder* "to be able"

PRESENT	PAST	FUTURE	IMPERATIVE
puedo	*pude*	*podré*	*puede* (fam.)
puedes	*pudiste*	*podrás*	*pueda* (pol.)
puede	*pudo*	*podrá*	*podamos*
			poded (fam.)
podemos	*pudimos*	*podremos*	*puedan* (pol.)
podéis	*pudisteis*	*podréis*	
pueden	*pudieron*	*podrán*	

¿Dónde puedo mandar   Where can I send a fax?
  un fax?
¿Podrás venir esta   Will you be able to
  noche?   come tonight?

LESSON 39

A. WHAT'S IN A NAME?

¿Cómo se llama él?
What's his name?

Se llama José Sánchez.
His name is Jose Sanchez.

¿Cómo se llama la señorita que está con él?
What's the name of the young lady with him?

Se llama María Suárez Navarro.
Her name is Maria Suarez Navarro.

¿Cómo se llama su padre?
What's her father's name?

Su padre se llama Antonio Suárez Coello.
Her father's name is Antonio Suarez Coello.

No me explico por qué ella se llama Navarro y su padre Coello.
I can't understand why her name is Navarro and her father's name is Coello.

Usted se equivoca. Ella no se llama Navarro, ni su padre Coello. Navarro y Coello son apellidos maternos, y no paternos.
You're wrong. Her name isn't Navarro and her father isn't Coello. Navarro and Coello are maternal not paternal surnames.

Perdóneme usted pero no entiendo. ¿Qué es eso de apellidos maternos y paternos?
Excuse me but I don't understand. What do you mean by maternal and paternal surnames?

Se lo explicaré a usted. Toda persona en España y en Hispanoamérica usa dos apellidos: el paterno y el materno.
I'll explain it to you. Everyone in Spain and in Latin America has two family names: the maternal and paternal.

¿Cómo es eso?
How come? ("How is this?")

Por ejemplo, el nombre de pila de esa señorita es María y sus apellidos son Suárez y Navarro. Suárez por su padre y Navarro por su madre. Así que ella se llama Señorita María Suárez Navarro.

For instance, the Christian ("baptismal") name of that young lady is Maria and her family names are Suarez and Navarro; Suarez for her father and Navarro for her mother. So her name is Miss Maria Suarez Navarro.

Ahora me doy cuenta. No es correcto llamar a una persona por su apellido materno.
Now I see. It's wrong to call a person by his maternal surname.

Exacto. Usted la puede llamar Señorita María Suárez Navarro o Señorita Suárez, pero nunca Señorita Navarro.
That's right. ("Exact.") You may call her Miss Maria Suarez Navarro or Miss Suarez, but never Miss Navarro.

¿Cómo se llama su madre?
What's her mother's name?

Su madre se llama Vicenta Navarro de Suárez.
Her mother's name is Vicenta Navarro de Suarez.

¿Por qué Navarro de Suárez?
Why Navarro de Suarez?

Pues, porque Navarro es su apellido de soltera y Suárez el de su marido.
Because Navarro is her maiden name and Suarez her husband's.

¿Cómo se dirige una carta a nombre de los dos?
How does one address a letter to them ("to the two")?

Usted debería escribir en el sobre "Señores Suárez Coello."

You should write on the envelope "Mr. and Mrs. Suarez Coello."

B. NOTES ON NAMES IN SPANISH

This complicated system has one advantage: it eliminates the need for the equivalent of our "junior." For example, If *Antonio Suárez Coello* names his son *Antonio*, and the mother's name is *Navarro*, the son's name is *Antonio Suárez Navarro* and so there is no need for a word like "junior" or "the second" to keep father and son apart.

If one brother whose family name is *Suárez Navarro* marries *Señorita Ruiz González* and another brother marries *Señorita García Pérez*, and each had a son named *José*, the two cousins sign themselves *José Suárez Ruiz* and *José Suárez García*. Sometimes only the first letter of the mother's name is written: *José Suárez R.* and *José Suárez G.*

A married woman keeps her maiden name and adds *de* followed by her husband's family name: *Navarro de Suárez*. Thus if *Señorita María Suárez Navarro* marries *Señor Alberto Sánchez* her name becomes *Señora María Suárez de Sánchez. De* ("of") before the husband's name stands for *esposa de* ("wife of").

LESSON 40

A. Fun in Spanish

UNA PERDIDA DE POCA IMPORTANCIA

A MINOR LOSS

—Señora, hágame el favor de darme *Interviú*. No tengo suelto.[1] ¿Puede usted cambiarme este billete?

—Ya me lo pagará usted mañana—dice la vendedora.

—¿Y si yo me muriera esta noche?

—¡Bah! No sería muy grande la pérdida.

"Madam, please give me a copy of *Interviú*. I haven't any change. Could you change this bill for me?"

"You can pay for it tomorrow," says the woman selling the newspaper.

"What if I should die tonight?"

"Oh, it wouldn't be a very great loss."

UNA LECCION DE ETIQUETA

A LESSON IN ETIQUETTE

Pedro y Juan van a comer a un restaurante. Los dos piden bistec. El camarero les sirve poco después. Pedro se apodera del bistec más grande. Juan, contrariado, le dice:

—¡Qué mal educado eres! Has sido el primero en servirte y has cogido el trozo más grande.

---

[1] Notice how Spanish punctuation in dialogues differs from English: (1) There are no quotation marks and (2) each change of speaker is indicated by a dash (see p. 251).

Pedro responde:
—*Estando tú en mi lugar, ¿qué pedazo hubieras cogido?*
—*El más pequeño, por supuesto.*
—*Entonces, ¿de qué te quejas? ¿No lo tienes ahí?*

Peter and John go to a restaurant to eat. They both ask for steak. The waiter brings the steaks to them shortly afterwards. Peter grabs the larger steak. John says to him angrily:

"What bad manners you have! You helped yourself first and you took the larger piece."

Peter answers:
"If you had been in my place, which piece would you have taken?"
"The smaller, of course."
"Then what are you complaining about? You have it, haven't you?"

NOTES

Pérdida loss.
De poca importancia of little importance.
Hágame el favor. Please. ("Do me the favor.")
Dar to give; *darme* to give me.
¿Puede usted? Can you?; from *poder* to be able (see p. 232).
Cambiar to change; *cambiarme* to change for me.
Ya already. Here it makes the sentence more expressive.
Pagará you will pay; from *pagar* to pay.
Dice he (she) says; from *decir* to say (see p. 228).
Vendedor merchant, storekeeper; *vendedora* (woman) shopkeeper.
Muriera should die; from *morir* to die.
Sería would be; from *ser* to be (see p. 291).

Esta noche ("this night") tonight.
Piden they ask for; from *pedir* to ask for.
Poco después a little afterwards, a little later.
Mal educado ill-bred.
Has cogido you *(fam.)* took; from *coger* to take.
Hubieras cogido would have taken.

UN OPTIMISTA

AN OPTIMIST

Mirando la solicitud, el jefe de una importante firma, abre los ojos con asombro cuando nota que el candidato, al empleo, que carecía de experiencia, pide un sueldo excesivo.

—¿No le parece—le preguntó al candidato,—que usted pide demasiado sueldo para la poca experiencia que tiene?

—Por el contrario—replicó el aspirante,—un trabajo del que no se sabe absolutamente nada es más difícil y debe pagarse mejor.

The head of an important firm, looking at an application, is astonished when he notices that the applicant, though lacking experience, asks for an excessive salary.

Rather puzzled, he asks him: "Doesn't it seem to you that you're asking for an excessive salary considering the little experience you have?"

"On the contrary," replies the applicant. "Work performed by one who knows nothing about it is harder and should be better paid."

NOTES

Mirando looking; from *mirar* to look.
Abre opens; from *abrir* to open.
Los ojos the eyes.

Con asombro with astonishment.

Nota he notes; from *notar* to note, see.

Carecía he lacked; from *carecer* to lack.

Pide asks for; from *pedir* to ask for (see p. 318).

No le parece doesn't it seem to you; from *parecer* to seem.

Preguntó he asked; from *preguntar* to ask.

Demasiado too much.

Un sueldo a salary.

Replicó he replied; from *replicar* to reply, answer.

El que no sabe (the) one who doesn't know; from *saber* to know (see p. 231).

No saber nada not to know anything.

EL ESPIRITU PRACTICO

THE PRACTICAL MIND

Un comerciante se presentó un día en casa de un campesino, pidiéndole que le procurara una libra de mantequilla. El campesino le contestó que se la daría a cambio de un par de calcetines de lana.

Cuando el comerciante se lo dijo a su mujer, ésta le dio la solución:

—Tenemos una colcha de lana—le dijo—, la desharé y haré un par de calcetines.

Así lo hizo, y el comerciante se llevó la libra de mantequilla, por la que dio el par de calcetines. Desde entonces, cuando el comerciante necesitaba mantequilla, su mujer deshacía un poco de la colcha y tejía unos calcetines. Pero llegó un día en que sólo tuvo lana para un calcetín. El comerciante se lo llevó al campesino, pidiéndole media libra de mantequilla.

—No—respondió el campesino—, le daré una libra. Mi mujer deshace los calcetines para una colcha que está casi terminando.

A merchant went to the house of a farmer and asked him if he could get him a pound of butter. The farmer said he would give it to him in exchange for a pair of woolen socks.

When the merchant told his wife about it, she suggested this solution: "We have a woolen quilt," she said. "I can unravel it and make a pair of socks."

She did so and the merchant got a pound of butter in exchange for the pair of socks. From then on, when the merchant needed butter, his wife unraveled some of the quilt and knitted socks. But one day there was just enough wool left to make one sock. The merchant took it to the farmer and asked him for half a pound of butter.

"No," said the farmer. "I'll give you a pound. My wife unravels the socks to make a quilt. All she needs is this one sock to finish it. . . ."

NOTES

El espíritu the spirit, mind.

Pidiéndole asking him; *pidiendo* asking; from *pedir* to ask; *le* him.

Procurara that he should get; from *procurar* to secure, get.

Daría that he would give; from *dar* to give.

Dijo he said, told; from *decir* to say, tell.

Dio he gave; from *dar* to give.

Desharé I will unravel; from *deshacer* to undo, unravel (*hacer* to do).

Hizo he did, made; from *hacer* to do, make.

Se llevó he carried or took away with him; from *llevarse* to carry or take away with one.

Llegó there came; from *llegar* to arrive.

Tuvo he had; from *tener* to have.

Daré I will give; from *dar* to give (see p. 333).

Que está casi terminando which she has almost finished. Or: *Mi mujer deshace los calcetines para hacer una colcha y sólo necesita un calcetín para terminarla.*

B. IMPORTANT SIGNS

Señores or *Hombres* or *Caballeros*	Men
Señoras or *Mujeres* or *Damas*	Women
Lavabo or *Lavatorio*	Lavatory
Cerrado	Closed
Abierto	Open
Prohibido fumar	No Smoking
Se prohibe la entrada	No Admittance
Llame/Toque	Knock
Toque el timbre	Ring
Privado	Private
Información dentro	Inquire within
¡Pare!	Stop!
¡Siga!	Go!
¡Cuidado!	Look out!
¡Peligro!	Danger!
¡Despacio!	Go slow!
Desvío	Detour
Precaución	Caution
Conserve su derecha	Keep to the right
Puente	Bridge
Prohibido el estacionamiento	No Parking
Consigna	Check Room
(oficina de) Cambio	Money Exchanged
Oficina de Información	Information
Sala de espera	Waiting Room
No asomarse (a la ventanilla)	Don't lean out (of the window)

Aeropuerto	Airport
Tren/Ferrocarril	Railroad
Expreso	Express
Local	Local
Parada	Stop (bus, train, etc.)
Prohibido fijar anuncios	Post No Bills
En reparación	Under Repair
Entrada	Entrance
Salida	Exit
Habitaciones amuebladas	Furnished Rooms
Departamentos/Pisos	Apartments
Recién pintado	Wet Paint
Cruce	Crossroads
Carnicería	Butcher ("Butcher's Shop")
Panadería	Bakery
Lechería	Dairy
Sastrería	Tailor Shop
Zapatería	Shoe Store
Peluquería, Barbería	Barber Shop
Mercado/Bodega/Ultramarinos	Grocer
Farmacia (Droguería, Botica)	Pharmacy, Drugstore
Confitería (Pastelería)	Confectioner, Candy Store
Papelería	Stationery Store
Buzón	Letter Box
Taberna	Saloon, Bar, Tavern
Comisaría	Police Station
Vinos	Wines
Gasolina	Gas Station
Librería	Book Store

Ayuntamiento	City Hall
Refrescos y bocadillos	Refreshments
(Agua) Fría	Cold (water)
(Agua) Caliente	Hot (water)

QUIZ 38

1. *Entrada*	a. No Smoking
2. *Desvío*	b. Express
3. *No asomarse (a la ventanilla)*	c. No Parking
4. *Cerrado*	d. Open
5. *Abierto*	e. Exit
6. *Prohibido fumar*	f. Information
7. *Expreso*	g. Detour
8. *Prohibido el estacionamiento*	h. Entrance
9. *Salida*	i. Closed
10. *Oficina de información*	j. Don't lean out (of the window)

ANSWERS
1—h; 2—g; 3—j; 4—i; 5—d; 6—a; 7—b; 8—c; 9—e; 10—f.

FINAL QUIZ
When you get 100% on this quiz you can consider that you have mastered the course.

1. ¿Me hace el favor de _____ (tell me) *dónde está la estación?*
   a. *permítame*
   b. *decirme*
   c. *tráigame*

2. ¿_____ (Can) *usted decirme dónde está la casa de correos?*
   a. *Puede*
   b. *Tiene*
   c. *Cuesta*

3. ¿Dónde _____ (is) *un buen restaurante?*
   a. *hace*
   b. *hay*
   c. *hoy*

4. _____ (Bring me) *un poco de pan.*
   a. *Conocerla*
   b. *Permítame*
   c. *Tráigame*

5. _____ (I need) *jabón.*
   a. *Necesito*
   b. *Tiene*
   c. *Permita*

6. _____ (I would like) *un poco más de carne.*
   a. *Tráigame*
   b. *Me hace falta*
   c. *Quisiera*

7. *Le* _____ (I introduce) *a mi amiga.*
   a. *Presento*
   b. *Tengo*
   c. *Venga*

8. ¿Dónde _____ (is) *el libro?*
   a. *está*
   b. *es*
   c. *este*

9. *Tenga* _____ (the goodness) *de hablar más despacio.*
    a. *la bondad*
    b. *el favor*
    c. *el gusto*

10. ¿_____ (Do you understand) *el español?*
    a. *Entiendo*
    b. *Habla usted*
    c. *Entiende usted*

11. _____ (Go) *allá.*
    a. *Vaya usted*
    b. *Habla usted*
    c. *Está usted*

12. _____ (Come) *en seguida.*
    a. *Venga*
    b. *Voy*
    c. *Vamos*

13. ¿*Cómo se* _____ (call) *usted?*
    a. *lava*
    b. *llama*
    c. *llamas*

14. ¿*Qué día de la* _____ (week) *es hoy?*
    a. *semana*
    b. *mes*
    c. *año*

15. ¿*Qué* _____ (time) *es?*
    a. *hora*
    b. *ahora*
    c. *tengo*

16. *No* _____ (I have) *cigarrillos.*
    a. *tiempo*
    b. *tengo*
    c. *tener*

17. *¿*_____ (Do you want) *algo de fruta?*
    a. *Podría usted*
    b. *Tiene usted*
    c. *Quiere usted*

18. _____ (Allow me) *que le presente a mi amigo.*
    a. *Déme*
    b. *Permítame*
    c. *Tráigame*

19. _____ (I'd like) *escribir una carta.*
    a. *Quiere*
    b. *Quisiera*
    c. *Permítame*

20. *¿Cuánto* _____ (costs) *un telegrama para Valencia?*
    a. *cuesta*
    b. *costar*
    c. *cuenta*

21. *Queremos* _____ (breakfast) *para tres personas.*
    a. *desayuno*
    b. *comida*
    c. *almuerzo*

22. *Es la* _____ (1:45).
    a. *una y treinta*
    b. *una y cuarenta y cinco*
    c. *una y quince*

23. *Venga* _____ (tomorrow morning).
   a. *ayer por la mañana*
   b. *mañana por la mañana*
   c. *mañana a mediodía*

24. *¿En qué* _____ (can I) *servirle?*
   a. *pueda*
   b. *puede*
   c. *puedo*

25. *No* _____ (has) *importancia.*
   a. *tenga*
   b. *tiene*
   c. *tenido*

ANSWERS
1—b; 2—a; 3—b; 4—c; 5—a; 6—c; 7—a; 8—a;
9—a; 10—c; 11—a; 12—a; 13—b; 14—a; 15—a;
16—b; 17—c; 18—b; 19—b; 20—a; 21—a; 22—b;
23—b; 24—c; 25—b.

SUMMARY OF SPANISH GRAMMAR

1. THE ALPHABET

LETTER	NAME	LETTER	NAME	LETTER	NAME
a	a	*j*	jota	*r*	ere
b	be	*k*	ka	*rr*	erre
c	c	*l*	ele	*s*	ese
				t	te
d	de	*m*	eme	*u*	u
e	e	*n*	ene	*v*	ve
f	efe	*ñ*	eñe	*w*	doble ve
g	ge	*o*	o	*x*	equis
h	hache	*p*	pe	*y*	i griega
i	i	*q*	cu	*z*	zeta

2. PRONUNCIATION

SIMPLE VOWELS

a   *ah*, like the *a* in f*a*ther
e   like the *ay* in d*ay*, but cut off sharply
i   like the *i* in mach*i*ne
o   like the *o* in *o*pen
u   like the *u* in r*u*le

VOWEL COMBINATIONS

ai } ay }	*ai* in *ai*sle.	ie io	*ye* in *ye*s. *yo* in *yo*ke.
au	*ou* in *ou*t.	ua	*wah*.
ei } ey }	*áy-ee*.	ou	*wo* in *wo*e.
eu	*áy-oo*	iu	*you*.
oi } oy }	*oy* in b*oy*.	ui } uy }	*óo-ee*.
ia	*ya* in *ya*rd.		

CONSONANTS

Notice the following points:

b, v   have the same sound. After a pause and after *m* or *n*, both are like *b* in *b*oy. When the sound occurs between vowels you bring the upper and lower lips together and blow between them, the way you do when blowing dust from something.[1]

c   before *o, a,* and *u,* and before consonants, is like *c* in *c*ut.

---

[1] Many Spanish speakers make the same difference between *b* and *v* that we do in English. They pronounce *b* whenever a *b* appears in the spelling and a *v* whenever a *v* appears in the spelling.

c	before *e* and *i* is pronounced in Spain like *th* in *thin*. In Spanish America it is pronounced like *s* in *see*.
ch	as in *church*.
d	after a pause or *n* and *l*, like *d*. When it occurs between vowels, like *th* in *that*.
g	before *a*, *o*, and *u*, and before consonants, after a pause, and after *n*, like *g* in *go*.
g	before *e* and *i* is a strong *h* as in *alcohol*.
h	is not pronounced.
j	is always like *g* before *e* and *i* (see above).
ll	is pronounced like *y* in *yes*.
ñ	is like *ni* in *onion* or *ny* in *canyon*.
qu	is like *k*.
r	is pronounced by tapping the tip of the tongue against the gum ridge back of the upper teeth.
rr	is trilled several times.
s	as in *see*.
x	before a consonant like *s;* between vowels like *x* *(ks)* in *extra*. Sometimes, however, it is like the *x (gs)* in *examine*.
y	when it begins a word or syllable, like *y* in *yes*.
y	when it serves as a vowel, like *i*.
z	is pronounced the same as the Spanish *c* before *e* and *i* (see above).

3. STRESS

1. Stress the last syllable if the word ends in a consonant other than *n* or *s*.

ciudad   city

2. Stress the next to the last syllable if the word ends in a vowel or *n* or *s*.

amigo   friend
hablan   they speak

3. Otherwise stress the syllable that has the accent (ˊ).

inglés   English
teléfono   telephone

4. PUNCTUATION

There are several differences between Spanish and English.

1. Exclamation and question marks precede as well as follow the sentence:

¿Adónde va usted?	Where are you going?
¡Hombre! ¿Adónde va Ud.?	Man! Where are you going?
¡Venga!	Come!
¡Qué hermoso día!	What a beautiful day!

2. The question mark is placed before the question part of the sentence:

Juan, ¿adónde vas?	John, where are you going?
Usted conoce al Sr. Díaz, ¿no es verdad?	You know Mr. Díaz, don't you?

3. Dashes are often used where we use quotation marks:

Muchas gracias—dijo.	"Thanks a lot," he said.
Esta mañana—dijo— *fui al centro.*	"This morning," he said, "I went downtown."
—¿Cómo está usted?	"How are you?"
—Muy bien, gracias.	"Very well, thank you."

4. Capitals are not used as frequently as in English. They are only used at the beginning of sentences and with proper nouns. *Yo* "I," adjectives of nationality, the days of the week and the months are not capitalized:

Somos americanos.	We're Americans.
El no es francés sino inglés.	He's not French but English.
Vendré el martes o el miércoles.	I'll come Tuesday or Wednesday.
Hoy es el primero de febrero.	Today is the first of February.

5. Suspension points (. . .) are used more frequently than in English to indicate interruption, hesitation, etc.

5. SOME ORTHOGRAPHIC SIGNS

1. The tilde (~) is used over the letter *n* to indicate the sound of *ni* in *onion* or *ny* in *canyon*.
2. The dieresis (¨) is used over *u* in the combination *gu*. It indicates that the vowel "u" is pronounced (gw).

vergüenza	shame
pingüino	penguin

6. THE DEFINITE ARTICLE

	SINGULAR	PLURAL
MASCULINE	*el*	*los*
FEMININE	*la*	*las*

SINGULAR

el muchacho	the boy
la muchacha	the girl

PLURAL

los muchachos	the boys
las muchachas	the girls

1. *El* is used before a feminine noun beginning with stressed *a* (or *ha*):

el agua	the water

But—

las aguas	the waters
el hacha	the axe

But—

las hachas	the axes

2. The neuter article *lo* is used before parts of speech other than nouns when they are used as nouns:

lo malo	what is bad, the bad part of it
lo hecho	what is done
lo dicho	what is said
lo útil	the useful

lo difícil   the difficult
lo posible   the possible
lo necesario the necessary

3. The definite article is used:

a. with abstract nouns:

La verdad vale más que   Truth is worth more than
    las riquezas.   riches.

b. with nouns referring to a class:

los soldados   soldiers
los generales   generals

c. with names of languages (except immediately
    after common verbs, such as *hablar, saber, apren-
    der, estudiar*, etc. or the prepositions *en* or *de*):

El español no es difícil.   Spanish is not difficult.
Habla bien el portugués.   She speaks Portuguese
                                                    well.

But—

Dígalo Ud. en inglés.   Say it in English.
Hablo español.   I speak Spanish.

d. in expressions of time:

la una   one o'clock
las dos   two o'clock
las diez   ten o'clock

e. for the days of the week:

Abren los domingos a   They open Sundays at
    las dos y media.   2:30.
el lunes próximo   next Monday

f. for the year, seasons, etc.

el año 1990	the year 1990
Vino el año pasado.	He came last year.
la primavera	spring
En el invierno hace frío.	It's cold in winter.

g. with certain geographical names:

El Brasil	Brazil
El Canadá	Canada
El Perú	Peru
El Uruguay	Uruguay
El Ecuador	Ecuador
El Japón	Japan

Note: The definite article is used with parts of the body and articles of clothing:

Me duele la cabeza.	My head hurts.
Quítese el abrigo.	Take your coat off.

7. THE INDEFINITE ARTICLE

	SINGULAR	PLURAL
MASCULINE	*un*	*unos*
FEMININE	*una*	*unas*

SINGULAR

un hombre	a man
una mujer	a woman
unos hombres	men, some (a few) men

PLURAL

unas mujeres	women, some (a few) women

1. *Unos (unas)* is often used where we use "some" or "a few" in English:

unos días   a few days

2. The indefinite article is omitted:

a. before rank, profession, trade, nationality, etc.:

Soy capitán.	I'm a captain.
Soy médico.	I'm a doctor.
Soy abogado.	I'm a lawyer.
Es profesor.	He's a teacher.
Soy norteamericano.	I'm an American.
Ella es española.	She's Spanish.

b. before *ciento* (or *cien*) "hundred," *cierto* "certain," *mil* "thousand":

cien hombres	a hundred men
cierto hombre	a certain man
mil hombres	a thousand men

c. in various idiomatic expressions, such as:

Salió sin sombrero.   He left without a hat.

8. CONTRACTIONS

1. de + el = del	of (from) the
del hermano	from (of) the brother
2. a + el = al	to the
al padre	to the father

9. THE DAYS OF THE WEEK

The days of the week are masculine and are not capitalized. The article is usually necessary, except after *ser*:

el domingo	Sunday
el lunes	Monday
el martes	Tuesday
el miércoles	Wednesday
el jueves	Thursday
el viernes	Friday
el sábado	Saturday
El domingo es el primer día de la semana.	Sunday is the first day of the week.
Van a visitarlos el domingo.	They're going to pay them a visit on Sunday.
Mañana es sábado.	Tomorrow is Saturday.

Notice that "on Sunday," "on Monday," etc., are *el domingo, el lunes;* "on Tuesdays," *los martes,* etc.

10. THE MONTHS OF THE YEAR

The names of the months are masculine and are not capitalized. They are usually used without the definite article:

enero	January
febrero	February
marzo	March
abril	April
mayo	May
junio	June
julio	July
agosto	August
septiembre	September
octubre	October
noviembre	November
diciembre	December

11. THE SEASONS

el invierno	winter
la primavera	spring
el verano	summer
el otoño	fall

The names of seasons are usually not capitalized. They are preceded by the definite article but after *de* and *en* the article may or may not be used:

Hace frío en (el) in-vierno.	It's cold in (the) winter.
Trabajo durante los me-ses de verano.	I work during the summer months.

12. MASCULINE AND FEMININE GENDER

Nouns referring to males are masculine; nouns referring to females are feminine:

el padre	the father	*la madre*	the mother
el hijo	the son	*la hija*	the daughter
el hombre	the man	*la mujer*	the woman
el toro	the bull	*la vaca*	the cow
el gato	the tomcat	*la gata*	the she-cat

The masculine plural of certain nouns stands for both genders:

los padres	the parents, the father and mother
los reyes	the king and queen
mis hermanos	my brothers and sisters

Masculine nouns and adjectives usually end in *-o;* feminine nouns and adjectives in *-a*.

1. Nouns ending in -*o* are usually masculine:

el cuerpo	the body
el cielo	the sky
el dinero	the money

Common Exceptions:

la mano	the hand
la radio/el radio	the radio

2. Nouns ending in *r, n,* and *l* are generally masculine:

el calor	the heat
el pan	the bread
el sol	the sun

3. Names of trees, days of the week, months, oceans, rivers, mountains, and other parts of speech used as nouns are generally masculine:

el álamo	the poplar
el martes	Tuesday
el Atlántico	The Atlantic Ocean
el Tajo	The Tagus River
los Andes	The Andes
el ser joven	being young, the fact of being young.

1. Nouns ending in -*a* (also -*dad, -tad, -tud, -ción, -sión, -ez, -umbre, -ie*) are usually feminine:

la cabeza	the head
la ciudad	the city
la cantidad	quantity
la libertad	liberty
la virtud	virtue
la condición	the condition
la costumbre	the custom
tensión	tension
madurez	maturity

Common Exceptions:

el día	the day
el mapa	the map
el drama	the drama
el clima	the climate
el problema	the problem
el poeta	the poet

2. Names of cities, towns, and fruits are generally feminine:

Barcelona es muy bonita.	Barcelona is very nice.
la naranja	the orange
la manzana	the apple

Note: Certain nouns differ in meaning depending on whether they take *el* or *la:*

el orden	order (arrangement)
el capital	capital (money)
el cura	priest

But—

la orden	order (command)
la capital	capital (city)
la cura	cure

13. THE PLURAL

1. Nouns ending in an unstressed vowel add -*s:*

el libro   the book   *los libros*   the books

2. Nouns ending in a consonant add -*es:*

el avión   the airplane
los aviones   the airplanes

3. Nouns ending in -*z* change the *z* to *c* and then add *es:*

la luz   the light   *las luces*   the lights
el lápiz the pencil   *los lápices*   the pencils

4. Some nouns are unchanged in the plural:

los martes   Tuesdays
los Martínez   the Martínez family

14. THE POSSESSIVE

English -'s or -s' is translated by *de* "of":

el libro de Juan   John's book ("the book
                            of John")
los libros de los niños   the boys' books ("the
                            books of the boys")

15. ADJECTIVES

1. Singular and Plural

SINGULAR

un muchacho alto	a tall boy
una muchacha alta	a tall girl

PLURAL

dos muchachos altos	two tall boys
dos muchachas altas	two tall girls

Notice that the adjective comes after the noun and is masculine if the noun is masculine, plural if the noun is plural, etc.

2. Feminine Endings

a. If the ending is *-o,* it becomes *-a:*

MASCULINE	FEMININE	
alto	*alta*	tall
rico	*rica*	rich
bajo	*baja*	low

b. In other cases there is no change:

MASCULINE	FEMININE	
grande	*grande*	big, large
azul	*azul*	blue
cortés	*cortés*	polite
útil	*útil*	useful
triste	*triste*	sad

Examples:

una cosa útil	a useful thing
una mujer triste	a sad woman
una muchacha cortés	a polite girl

c. Adjectives of nationality add *-a* or change *o* to *a:*

MASCULINE	FEMININE	
español	*española*	Spanish
francés	*francesa*	French
inglés	*inglesa*	English
americano	*americana*	American

Examples:

una señora inglesa	an English woman
la lengua española	the Spanish language

d. Adjectives ending in *-án* or *-ón*[1] and *-or* add *-a:*

MASCULINE	FEMININE	
holgazán	*holgazana*	lazy
burlón	*burlona*	jesting
preguntón	*preguntona*	inquisitive
encantador	*encantadora*	charming
fascinador	*fascinadora*	fascinating

3. The following adjectives drop the final *-o* when they come before a masculine singular noun:

uno	one
bueno	good
malo	bad
alguno	some one
ninguno	no one
primero	first
tercero	third

Examples:

un buen amigo	a good friend
ningún hombre	no man

[1] Notice that the accent is dropped in the feminine.

| *el mal tiempo* | the bad weather |
| *el primer día* | the first day |

4. *Grande* becomes *gran* when it comes before a singular noun:

un gran amigo	a great friend
un gran poeta	a great poet
un gran hombre	a great (important) man

But—

| *un hombre grande* | a large (tall) man |

5. *Santo* becomes *San* when it comes before a noun (except those beginning in *To-* and *Do-*):

| *San Juan* | Saint John |
| *San Luis* | Saint Louis |

But—

| *Santo Tomás* | Saint Thomas |
| *Santo Domingo* | Saint Dominic |

6. *Ciento* becomes *cien* before a noun and the number *mil:*

| *cien dólares* | a hundred dollars |
| *cien mil personas* | one hundred thousand people |

16. POSITION OF ADJECTIVES

1. Descriptive adjectives usually follow the noun:

un libro blanco	a white book
una casa blanca	a white house
mi sombrero nuevo	my new hat
dinero español	Spanish money
un hombre inteligente	an intelligent man
huevos frescos	fresh eggs

2. Exceptions are adjectives which describe an inherent quality:

un buen muchacho	a good boy

3. Articles, numerals, possessives, and quantitatives usually precede the noun:

muchas personas	many persons
poca gente	few people
cuatro huevos	four eggs
mis libros	my books

4. Some descriptive adjectives can come either before or after the noun:

una niña pequeña or *una pequeña niña*	a little girl
un día hermoso or *un hermoso día*	a nice (beautiful) day
una linda muchacha or *una muchacha linda*	a pretty girl

Other common adjectives used this way are *bueno* "good," *malo* "bad," and *bonito* "pretty."

5. A few adjectives have one meaning when they come before a noun and another when they follow:

un hombre pobre	a poor man
¡Pobre hombre!	Poor man!
un hombre grande	a large (tall) man
un gran hombre	a great (important) man
un libro nuevo	a new (recent) book
un nuevo hombre	a different man
cierto hombre	a certain man
una noticia cierta	a true piece of news

17. COMPARISON

1. Regular Comparison

fácil	easy
más fácil	easier
menos fácil	less easy
el más fácil	the easiest
el menos fácil	the least easy

2. Irregular Comparison

bueno	good	*mejor*	better, best
malo	bad	*peor*	worse, worst
mucho	much	*más*	more, most
poco	little	*menos*	less, least
grande	great	{ *mayor* / *más grande*	
pequeño	small	{ *menor* / *más pequeño*	

Más grande means "larger," "bigger"; *mayor* means "older":

Esta mesa es más grande que aquélla.	This table is larger than that one.

Pedro es mayor que   Peter is older than John.
Juan.

    Similarly, *más pequeño* means "smaller"; *menor* means "younger."

3. "More (less) . . . than . . ." = *más (menos) . . . que . . .*

El español es más fácil   Spanish is easier than
que el inglés.   English.
Es más inteligente de lo   He's more intelligent
que parece.   than he looks.

4. "As . . . as . . ." = *tan . . . como . . .* or *tanto . . . como . . .*
   a. before an adjective or adverb:

Tan fácil como . . .   As easy as . . .
El habla español tan   He speaks Spanish as
bien como yo.   well as I do.

   b. before a noun:

Tiene tanto dinero como He has as much money
Ud.   as you.

5. "The more (less) . . . the more (less) . . ." = *cuanto más (menos) . . . tanto más (menos) . . .*

Cuanto más le trate   The more you get to
  tanto más le agra-   know him (deal with
  dará.   him) the more you
             like him.

6. "Most" = *-ísimo* (absolute superlative)

| *Es muy útil.* | It's very useful. |
| *Es utilísimo.* | It's most useful. |

18. PRONOUNS

Pronouns have different forms depending on whether they are:

1. the subject of a verb
2. used after a preposition
3. the direct object of a verb
4. used as indirect objects
5. used with reflexive verbs

1. Pronouns as the subject of a verb:

SINGULAR

yo	I
tú	you
él	he
ella	she
usted	you *(polite)*

PLURAL

nosotros	we *(masc.)*
nosotras	we *(fem.)*
vosotros	you *(masc.)*
vosotras	you *(fem.)*
ellos	they *(masc.)*
ellas	they *(fem.)*
ustedes	you *(polite)*

SINGULAR

(yo) hablo	I speak
(tú) hablas	you speak *(familiar)*
(él) habla	he speaks

| *(ella) habla* | she speaks |
| *(usted) habla* | you speak *(polite)* |

PLURAL

(nosotros) hablamos	we speak *(masc.)*
(nosotras) hablamos	we speak *(fem.)*
(vosotros) habláis	you speak *(masc.)*
(vosotras) habláis	you speak *(fem.)*
(ellos) hablan	they speak *(masc.)*
(ellas) hablan	they speak *(fem.)*
(ustedes) hablan	you speak *(polite)*

The personal pronouns *yo, tú,* etc., are not ordinarily used. "I speak" is just *hablo,* "we speak," *hablamos,* etc. They are used for emphasis or clearness (*usted habla* "you speak" and *él habla* "he speaks").

2. Pronouns used after prepositions:

para mí	for me
para ti	for you *(fam.)*
para él	for him
para ella	for her
para usted	for you *(polite)*
para nosotros	for us *(masc.)*
para nosotras	for us *(fem.)*
para vosotros	for you *(masc.)*
para vosotras	for you *(fem.)*
para ellos	for them *(masc.)*
para ellas	for them *(fem.)*
para ustedes	for you *(polite)*

Notice that the form of the pronoun used after a preposition is the same as the form of the pronoun used before a verb, except for *mí* "me" and *ti* "you" *(fam.).*

There is a special form for "with me," "with you" and "with him": *conmigo* "with me," *contigo* "with you" and *consigo* "with him."

3. Pronouns as direct objects:

me	me
te	you *(fam.)*
le	him, you *(polite)* (used only in Spain)
la	her, you, it *(fem.)*
lo	him, you, it *(masc.)*
nos	us
os	you *(fam.)*
los	them, you *(polite)*
las	them, you *(fem.)*

4. Pronouns as indirect objects:

me	to me
te	to you *(fam.)*
le	to him, her, you *(polite)*
nos	to us
os	to you *(fam.)*
les	to them *(masc.* and *fem.)*
	to you *(masc.* and *fem.)* *(polite)*

Le as indirect object means "to him," "to her," "to you" (usted), and *les* means "to them," "to you" (ustedes). The preposition *a* and the prepositional forms *él, ella, usted* and *ellos, ellas, ustedes* are often added for clearness.

SHORT FORM

le doy	=	I give to him
		I give to her
		I give to you
les doy	=	I give to them *(masc.)*
		I give to them *(fem.)*
		I give to you

FULL FORM

le doy a él	I give (to) him
le doy a ella	I give (to) her
le doy a usted	I give (to) you
les doy a ellos	I give (to) them
les doy a ellas	I give (to) them
les doy a ustedes	I give (to) you

This double construction is used even when the object is a noun:

Le escribí a María ayer.   I wrote to Mary yesterday.

5. Reflexive pronouns:
   Reflexive pronouns are used when a person (or thing) does something to himself, herself (or itself); e.g., "I wash myself."

me	myself
te	yourself *(fam.)*
se	himself, herself, yourself *(polite)*
nos	ourselves
os	yourselves *(fam.)*
se	themselves, yourselves *(polite)*

For examples, see pp. 84 and 85.

19. POSITION OF PRONOUNS

1. When there are both direct and indirect object pronouns in a sentence *(he gives it to me)* the Spanish order is the following:

	ENGLISH			SPANISH		
	1	*2*		*2*	*1*	
He gives	it	to	me.	*Me*	*lo*	*da*
	1	*2*		*2*	*1*	
They give	it	to	us.	*Nos*	*lo*	*dan.*

That is, the indirect pronoun precedes the direct. If both begin with *l*, the indirect *(le, les)* becomes *se:*

Se lo diré (instead of *le lo diré*).	I will tell it to him (to her, to you, etc.)

2. When *se* is present it comes before the other object pronouns. It denotes:

a. an impersonal action:

Se dice.	It is said.
Se la trató bien.	She was treated well.

b. a personal object (may or may not be reflexive):

Se lo dice.	He says it to him (her) *or* he says it to himself *or* she says it to herself.

3. If *se* is not present, the first pronoun of the group has the meaning of an indirect object and the second that of a direct object:

Me lo da.   He gives it to me.

4. Object pronouns come before the verb:

Lo veo.   I see him.
Se lo da.   He gives it to him.

They come after an infinitive or present participle:

Tenerlo.   To have it.
Dárselo.   To give it to him.
Quiero verlo.   I want to see him.
Voy a verlo.   I'm going to see him.
Teniéndolo.   Having it.
Diciéndolo.   Saying it.
Estoy mirándolo.   I am looking at him.

Object pronouns follow affirmative commands:

Tómalo.   Take it.
Dígamelo Ud.   Tell it to me.

They come before negative commands (these are always in the subjunctive):

No me lo diga Ud.   Don't tell me.

5. *Te* and *os* precede all pronouns except *se:*

Te lo diré.   I will tell it to you.

But—

Se te dijo.   It was told to you.

20. Conjunctions

y	and
o	or
pero	but
mas	but
que	that
pues	since, as
si	if
por qué	why
porque	because
ni . . . ni	neither . . . nor

NOTES

a. *y* "and"

Roberto y Juan son hermanos.	Robert and John are brothers.

e is used instead of *y* before a word beginning with *i-* or *hi-:*

María e Isabel son primas.	Mary and Elizabeth are cousins.
Madre e hija.	Mother and daughter.

b. *o* "or"

Cinco o seis pesos.	Five or six pesos.
Voy con mi hermano o con mi hermana.	I'm going with my brother or with my sister.

u is used instead of *o* before a word beginning with *o-* or *ho-:*

Siete u ocho horas.	Seven or eight hours.
Cinco u ocho meses.	Five or eight months.

c. *pero* "but"

Quiero venir pero no puedo.	I want to come but I can't.

d. *mas* "but" is more formal and literary:

Pensé que vendría mas no pudo.	I thought he would come but he wasn't able to.

e. *sino* "but is used instead of *pero* after a negative statement:

No es francés sino inglés.	He is not French but English.
No viene hoy sino mañana.	He is not coming today but tomorrow.

21. QUESTION WORDS

1. *¿Qué?* — What?
   ¿Qué dice usted? — What are you saying?
2. *¿Por qué?* — Why?
   ¿Por qué dice usted eso? — Why do you say that?
3. *¿Cómo?* — How?
   ¿Cómo se dice en español esto? — How do you say this in Spanish?
   ¿Cómo se llama usted? — What's your name? ("How do you call yourself?")
4. *¿Cuánto?* — How much?

¿Cuánto dinero necesita usted?	How much money do you need?
¿Cuántos libros hay?	How many books are there?
¿Cuánto hay de Madrid a Barcelona?	How far is it from Madrid to Barcelona?

5. *¿Cuál?* — What? Which one?
   ¿Cuál es su nombre? — What's your name?
   ¿Cuál quiere usted? — Which one do you want?

6. *¿Quién?* — Who?
   ¿Quién vino con usted? — Who came with you?
   ¿Quién tiene eso? — Who has that?

7. *¿Dónde?* — Where?
   ¿Dónde está su amigo? — Where is your friend?

8. *¿Cuándo?* — When?
   ¿Cuándo se marcha Ud? — When are you going (leaving)?
   ¿Cuándo ocurrió eso? — When did that happen?

Notice that the question words are written with an accent.

22. ADVERBS

1. Spanish *-mente* corresponds to "*-ly*" in English. It is added to the feminine form of the adjective:

exclusivamente   exclusively

When there are two adverbs, the ending *-mente* is added only to the last one:

clara y concisamente   clearly and concisely

Adverbs are compared like adjectives.

POSITIVE	*alegremente*	cheerfully
COMPARATIVE	*más alegremente*	more cheerfully
SUPERLATIVE	*ló más alegremente*	most cheerfully

2. Irregular Comparatives:

POSITIVE		COMPARATIVE	
bien	well	*mejor*	better, best
mal	badly	*peor*	worse, worst
mucho	much	*más*	more, most
poco	little	*menos*	less, least

3. Adverbs as prepositions or conjunctions. Many adverbs act as prepositions when *de* is added:

ADVERB:	*después*	afterward
PREPOSITION:	*después de las cinco*	after five o'clock
ADVERB:	*además*	besides
PREPOSITION:	*además de*	besides

When *que* is added they act as conjunctions:

después de que venga   after he comes

Other words which act similarly: *antes* "before"; *cerca* "near"; *delante* "before," "in front of"; *enfrente* "opposite."

4. Adverbs of time:

hoy	today
ayer	yesterday
mañana	tomorrow
temprano	early

tarde	late
a menudo	often
siempre	always
nunca	never
jamás	never
luego	afterward
rápido	quickly
despacio	slowly
antes que	before
después	afterward

5. Adverbs of place:

aquí	here
acá	here (motion)
ahí	there
allí	there (farther away)
adelante	forward, on
atrás	behind
dentro	inside
arriba	up, above
fuera	outside
abajo	down, below
cerca	near
lejos	far

6. Adverbs of quantity:

muy	very
mucho	much
poco	little
más	more
menos	less
además	besides
cuánto	how much
tan	so much

tanto	so much
demasiado	too much
apenas	scarcely

7. Adverbs expressing affirmation:

sí	yes
verdaderamente	truly
cierto	certainly
ciertamente	certainly
claro	of course
desde luego	of course
por supuesto	of course

8. Adverbs expressing negation:

no	no, not
nunca	never
jamás	never
nunca jamás	never (more emphatic)
ya no	no more, not now
todavía no	not yet
tampoco	neither, either
no tal	no indeed
ni	nor
ni . . . ni	neither . . . not
ni siquiera	not even

9. Here and There:
   Aquí "here" refers to something near the speaker:

Tengo aquí los libros.   I have the books here.

   Ahí "there" refers to something near the person spoken to:

¿Qué tiene Ud. ahí?	What do you have there?
¿Está Ud. ahí?	Are you there?

Acá "here" expresses motion toward the speaker:

¡Venga Ud. acá! Come here!

Allá "there" indicates motion away from the speaker:

¡Vaya Ud. allá!	Go there!
Va allá.	He's going there.

Allí "there" refers to something remote from both:

Vienen de allí.	They come from there.
Viví en Sudamérica por varios años. ¿Ha estado Ud. allí?	I've lived in South America for several years. Have you ever been there?

23. DIMINUTIVES AND AUGMENTATIVES

The endings *-ito (-cito, -ecito)*, *-illo (-cillo, -ecillo)*, *-uelo (-zuelo, -ezuelo)* imply smallness. In addition, *-ito* often implies attractiveness or admiration, *-illo* and *-uelo* unattractiveness or depreciation. (They should be used with care.)

chico	boy	*chiquillo*	little boy
señora	lady, Mrs.	*señorita*	young lady, Miss
un poco	a little	*un poquito*	a little bit
pedazo	piece	*pedacito*	a little piece
gato	cat	*gatito*	kitten

papá	papa	*papito*	daddy
cuchara	tablespoon	*cucharita*	teaspoon
Venecia	Venice	*Venezuela*	Venezuela ("little Venice")
cigarro	cigar	*cigarrillo*	cigarette
autor	author	*autorcillo*	unimportant author

The endings *-ón (ona)* and *-ote* indicate largeness (often awkwardness and unattractiveness as well):

tonto	foolish, silly fool	*tontón*	big fool
silla	chair	*sillón*	big chair
cuchara	spoon	*cucharón*	a ladle
hombre	man	*hombrón*	he-man

24. DEMONSTRATIVES

1. Demonstrative Adjectives:

MASCULINE	FEMININE	
este	*esta*	this
ese	*esa*	that
aquel	*aquella*	that (farther removed)
estos	*estas*	these
esos	*esas*	those
aquellos	*aquellas*	those (farther removed)

a. Spanish demonstrative adjectives usually precede the nouns they modify and always agree in gender and number:

este muchacho	this boy
aquellos vecinos	those neighbors

b. *Ese* and *aquel* both mean "that." *Aquel* points out a thing removed in space or time from the speaker or from the person spoken to:

Esa señora es muy amable.	That lady is very kind.
Aquel señor que llegó el mes pasado.	That gentleman who arrived last month.

2. Demonstrative Pronouns:

MASCULINE	FEMININE	
éste	*ésta*	this (one)
ése	*ésa*	that (one)
aquél	*aquélla*	that (one)
éstos	*éstas*	these
ésos	*ésas*	those
aquéllos	*aquéllas*	those

NEUTER	
esto	this (one)
eso	that (one)
aquello	that (one)

The same difference exists between the pronouns *ése* and *aquél* as between the adjectives *ese* and *aquel*:

No quería éste sino aquél.	I didn't want this one but the one over there.

Este and *aquél* also mean "the latter" and "the former":

Acaban de llegar el embajador y su secretario.	The ambassador and his secretary just arrived.
Este es joven y aquél es viejo.	The former is old and the latter is young.

Notice that the Spanish order is the opposite of the English: *éste . . . aquél* ("the latter . . . the former").

The neuter demonstrative pronouns *esto, eso,* and *aquello* refer to an idea previously stated and not to a specific thing:

Me dijo que aquello fue horrible.	He told me that that was horrible.

25. INDEFINITE ADJECTIVES AND PRONOUNS

todos	all
tal	such
ni uno	not one
otro	other
alguien	someone
nadie	nobody
algo	something, anything
ninguno	no one, none
alguno	someone
varios	several
nada	nothing
cualquiera	whatever, whoever
quienquiera	whoever

26. NEGATION

1. *No* "not" comes before the verb:

No veo.	I don't see.
Él no habla.	He isn't speaking.

2. There are two forms for "nothing," "never," "no one," etc.—one with and one without *no:*

No veo nada.	I see nothing.
No voy nunca.	I never go.
No viene nadie.	No one is coming.

Or—

Nada veo.	I see nothing.
Nunca voy.	I never go.
Nadie viene	No one comes.

27. WORD ORDER

1. The usual order is subject–verb–adverb–object:

Juan vio allí a sus amigos.	John saw his friends there.

2. The tendency in Spanish is to put the longer member of the sentence or the emphasized part last:

Me dio una carta.	He gave me a letter.
¿Compró la casa su padre?	Did your father buy the house?
Han caído veinte soldados.	Twenty soldiers were killed.

3. As in English, questions sometimes have the same order as statements but with the question intonation (that is, with a rise in pitch at the end):

¿Juan va a ir allí?   John is going to go there?

4. However, the more usual way of asking a question is to put the subject after the verb:

¿Va a ir allí Juan?	Is John going to go there?
¿Viene su amigo?	Is your friend coming?
¿Ha comido Ud.?	Have you eaten?
¿Habla usted español?	Do you speak Spanish?
¿Tiene usted dinero?	Do you have any money?
¿Por qué volvió Ud.?	Why did you return?
¿Ha recibido Juan mi carta?	Did John get my letter?

5. Adjectives come right after *ser:*

¿Es tarde?	Is it late?
¿Es bueno?	Is it good?
¿Es difícil la prueba?	Is the test difficult?
¿Es fácil el problema?	Is the problem easy?

28. TENSES OF THE VERB

Spanish verbs are divided into three clauses ("conjugations") according to their infinitives:

Class I—*hablar*
Class II—*comer*
Class III—*vivir*

1. The Present:

I	II	III
-o	-o	-o
-as	-es	-es
-a	-e	-e
-amos	-emos	-imos
-áis	-éis	-ís
-an	-en	-en

hablar to speak *comer* to eat *vivir* to live

hablo	como	vivo
hablas	comes	vives
habla	come	vive

hablamos	comemos	vivimos
habláis	coméis	vivís
hablan	comen	viven

The following verbs insert *g* in the first person singular of the present indicative:

tener—tengo	I have
venir—vengo	I come
traer—traigo	I bring
poner—pongo	I put
hacer—hago	I do
decir—digo	I say
salir—salgo	I leave

The present can be translated in several ways:

Hablo español.	I speak Spanish.
	I am speaking Spanish.
	I do speak Spanish.

2. The Imperfect:

I	II AND III
-aba	*-ía*
-abas	*-ías*
-aba	*-ía*
-ábamos	*-íamos*
-abais	*-íais*
-aban	*-ían*

a. The imperfect is used:

1. to indicate continued or customary action in the past:

Cuando yo estaba en Madrid, siempre visitaba los teatros.	When I was in Madrid, I always used to visit the theaters.
Le encontraba todos los días.	I used to meet him every day.

2. to indicate what was happening when something else happened:

Él escribía cuando ella entró.	He was writing when she entered.

b. Irregular Imperfects:
The following are the only Spanish verbs which are irregular in the imperfect:
ser—era, eras, era, éramos, érais, eran
ir—iba, ibas, iba, íbamos, íbais, iban
ver—veía, veías, veía, veíamos, veíais, veían

3. The Future:
The future of regular verbs is formed by adding to the infinitive ending *-é, -ás, -á, -emos, -éis, -án:*

hablar to speak	*comer* to eat	*vivir* to live
hablaré	*comeré*	*viviré*
hablarás	*comerás*	*vivirás*
hablará	*comerá*	*vivirá*
hablaremos	*comeremos*	*viviremos*
hablaréis	*comeréis*	*viviréis*
hablarán	*comerán*	*vivirán*

The future generally expresses a future action:

Lo compraré.	I'll buy it.
Iré mañana.	I'll go tomorrow.

Sometimes it expresses probability or conjecture:

¿Qué hora será?	What time can it be? What time do you think it must be?
Será la una.	It must be almost one.
Estará comiendo ahora.	He's probably eating now.

4. The Preterite:
There are two sets of preterite endings:

a. One set is used with the stem of Conjugation I *(-ar):*

- -é
- -aste
- -ó
- -amos
- -asteis
- -aron

b. The other set is used with the stem of Conjugation II *(-er)* and Conjugation III *(-ir):*

- -í
- -iste
- -ió
- -imos
- -isteis
- -ieron

The preterite expresses an action that began in the past and ended in the past:

Él lo dijo.	He said it.
Habló conmigo.	He spoke with me.
Fui allí.	I went there.
Él nos vio.	He saw us
Escribí una carta.	I wrote a letter.
Llovió todo el día.	It rained all day.
El tren se paró.	The train stopped.
Pasó tres años allí.	He spent three years there.
Lo vi.	I saw him (it).

5. The Present Perfect:
   The present perfect is formed by adding the past participle to the present tense of *haber*. It is used to indicate a past action which continues into the present or which ended only recently:

Ha venido con su amigo.	He has come with his friend.
Nos ha escrito.	He has written to us.

6. The Pluperfect:
   The pluperfect is formed by adding the past participle to the imperfect of *haber*. It translates the English pluperfect:

Ya habían llegado.	They had already arrived.

7. The Future Perfect:
   The future perfect is formed by adding the past participle to the future of *haber*. It translates the English future perfect:

| *Habrán llegado para entonces.* | They will have arrived by then. |

Sometimes it indicates probability:

| *Habrán llegado ayer.* | They probably arrived yesterday. |

8. The Preterite Perfect:
The preterite perfect, which is rather rare, is formed by adding the past participle to the preterite of *haber*. It is used to indicate that something has occurred immediately before some other action in the past:

| *Apenas hubo oído eso, se marchó.* | No sooner had he heard that than he left. |

29. CONDITIONAL

1. The conditional of all verbs is formed by adding to the infinitive the endings: *ía, ías, ía, íamos, íais, ían.* It translates the English "would."

I	II	III
hablar to speak	*comer* to eat	*vivir* to live
hablaría	*comería*	*viviría*
hablarías	*comerías*	*vivirías*
hablaría	*comería*	*viviría*
hablaríamos	*comeríamos*	*viviríamos*
hablaríais	*comeríais*	*viriríais*
hablarían	*comerían*	*vivirían*

Sometimes it expresses probability or conjecture:

Serían las dos cuando él llegó.	It was probably about two o'clock when he arrived.
¿Qué hora sería?	What time could it have been?

2. The perfect conditional is formed by adding the past participle to the conditional of *haber*. It translates the English "would have."

Habría hablado.	I would have spoken.
Habría ido.	I would have gone.

3. If a sentence contains a clause beginning with *si* "if," the tense of the verb is determined by the tense of the verb in the main clause.

If the main clause has a verb in the:	The "if" clause has a verb in the:
Present	Present/Future
Future	Present
Imperfect	Imperfect
Preterite	Preterite
Conditional	Imp. Subjunctive (-*ra* or -*se*)
Si está aquí, trabaja.	If he is here, he is working.
Si estaba aquí, trabajaba.	If he was here, he was working.
Si está aquí mañana, trabajará.	If he's here tomorrow, he'll be working.
Si estuviera aquí, trabajaría.	If he were here, he'd be working.

30. SUBJUNCTIVE

The indicative simply makes a statement; the subjunctive indicates a certain attitude toward the statement—uncertainty, desire, emotion, etc. The subjunctive is used in subordinate clauses when the statement is unreal, doubtful, indefinite, subject to some condition, or is affected by will, emotion, etc.

1. Forms

a. The subjunctive endings of the second and third conjugations are the same.

b. The present subjunctive is formed by adding the subjunctive endings to the stem of the first person singular, present indicative; the imperfect subjunctive, by adding the endings of the stem of the third person plural, preterite.

The subjunctive endings are as follows:

Conjugation I

PRES. SUBJ.   *-e, -es, -e, -emos, -éis, -en*
IMPERF. SUBJ. *-ara, -aras, -ara, -áramos, -arais,*
               -aran
               Or—
               -ase, -ases, -ase, -ásemos, -aseis,
               -asen

Conjugations II and III

PRES. SUBJ.   *-a, -as, -a, -amos, -ís, -an*
IMPERF. SUBJ. *-iera, -ieras, -iera, -iéramos,*
               -ierais, -ieran
               Or—
               -iese, -ieses, -iese, -iésemos,
               -ieseis, -iesen

	I	II	III
INFINITIVE	*hablar*	*comer*	*vivir*
PRES. SUBJ.	*hable*	*coma*	*viva*
IMPERF.	*hablara*	*comiera*	*viviera*
SUBJ.	*hablase*	*comiese*	*viviese*

2. Uses

a. The subjunctive is used with verbs of desire, request, suggestion, permission, approval and disapproval, judgment, opinion, uncertainty, emotion, surprise, fear, denial, etc.:

Quisiera verlo.	I'd like to see him.
¡Ojalá que lo haga!	I wish he would do it!
¡Ojalá lo supiera!	I wish I knew it!
Temo que se lo diga a él.	I'm afraid he may tell it to him.
No creo que él le haya visto.	I don't believe he's seen him.
Niega que le haya visto.	He denies that he's seen him.
Me sorprende mucho que él no lo haya hecho.	I'm greatly surprised that he hasn't done it.
Espero que no venga.	I hope he doesn't come.
Me alegro de que Ud. esté aquí.	I'm glad you're here!
Temo que esté enfermo.	I'm afraid he's sick.
Temo que no llegue a tiempo.	I'm afraid he won't (may not) come in time.
Duda que lo hagamos.	He doubts that we'll do it.

Dudo que sea verdad.	I doubt that it's true.
Dudo que sea posible.	I doubt whether it's possible.
No creo que lo sepa.	I don't think he knows it.
Se lo digo para que lo sepa.	I'm telling you so you may know it.

b. The subjunctive forms are used in commands: Affirmative or negative commands in the polite form:

¡Abra usted la ventana!	Open the window!
¡No hablen ustedes ahora!	Don't talk now!

1. Negative commands in the familiar form:

No me digas (tú).	Don't tell me!
No habléis ahora.	Don't talk now!

2. Suggestions in which the speaker is included:

Leamos.	Let's read!
Entremos.	Let's go in!

3. Indirect commands (that is, commands in the third person):

Que vaya él.	Let him go.
¡Viva España!	Long live Spain!
¡Que vengan!	Let them come!
¡Que entren!	Let them come in!
¡Que no venga!	Let him not come!

c. The subjunctive is used in conditional sentences which are contrary to fact:

Si estaba allí, yo no le vi.	If he was there, I didn't see him. *(Indicative)*
No iremos si llueve.	If it rains, we won't go. *(Indicative)*

But—

Si fuera él, lo haría.	If I were him (he), I'd do it.
Si fuera mío esto, lo vendería.	If this were mine, I'd sell it.
Si tuviera el dinero, lo compraría.	If I had the money, I'd buy it.
Aunque hubiese tenido dinero no hubiera ido.	Even if I had had the money I wouldn't have gone.
Si lo hubiera sabido, no habría venido.	If I had known it, I wouldn't have come.
Si hubiese estado aquí, habríamos ido.	If he had been here, we would have gone.
Aunque lo hubiese intentado, no hubiera podido hacerlo.	Even if I would have tried, I wouldn't have been able to do it.

d. The subjunctive is used after impersonal verbs which do not express certainty:

Es importante que vengan.	It's important for them to come.
Es preciso que estén aquí.	It's necessary for them to be here.
Es necesario que Ud. venga.	It's necessary that you come.
Es posible que lo tenga.	It's possible that he has it.

Era lástima que no   It was a pity that they
   vinieran.   didn't come.

e. The subjunctive is used after various conjunctive
   adverbs:

1. Certain conjunctive adverbs are always followed
   by the subjunctive because they never introduce
   statements of accomplished fact:

antes (de) que	before
a condición de	on condition that
aunque	even if
a (fin de) que	in order that
a menos que	unless
como si	as if
con tal (de) que	provided that, providing
dado que	granted that, given . . .
no obstante que	notwithstanding that
supuesto que	supposing that

2. Other conjunctive adverbs may or may not introduce a statement of accomplished fact. When
   they do, they take the indicative; otherwise the
   subjunctive:

a menos que	unless
a pesar de que	in spite of, notwith-standing
antes que	before
así que	as soon as
aunque	although, even though
con tal que	provided (that)
cuando	when
de manera que	so that
de modo que	so that

después (de) que	after
en cuanto	as soon as
hasta que	until
luego que	as soon as
mientras que	as long as, while
para que	in order that, so that
siempre que	provided that, whenever
Aunque él no lo quiera, se lo daré.	I'll give it to him even though he may not want it.
Lo compraré aunque me cueste mucho.	I'll buy it even if it costs me a lot.
Se lo digo para que lo sepa.	I'm telling you so that you may know it.
Aunque llueva mañana.	Although it may rain tomorrow.
Se fue sin que lo supiésemos.	He went away without our knowing it.
Iré con Ud. con tal que tenga tiempo.	I'll go with you provided I have time.
En caso que llegue.	In case he arrives.

Compare:

Iremos aunque llueve.	We'll go even though it's raining.
Iremos aunque llueva.	We'll go even if it rains (even if it should rain).

f. The subjunctive is used when an indefinite antecedent expresses doubt or denial about a person's existence.:

No hay ningún hombre que entienda esto.	There is no man who understands this.

Busco a alguien que hable español.	I'm looking for someone who speaks Spanish.
No conozco a nadie que pueda hacerlo.	I don't know anyone who can do it (could do it).

g. The subjunctive is used after compounds of *-quiera* "-ever": *quienquiera* "whoever," *dondequiera* "wherever," *cualquier* "whatever," "whichever":

Quienquiera que sea.	Whoever he (it) may be.
Él quiere hacer cualquier cosa que ella haga.	He wants to do whatever she does.
Él quiere ir dondequiera que ella vaya.	He wants to go wherever she goes.

31. COMMANDS AND REQUESTS (THE IMPERATIVE)

There are two types of commands, one with *tú*, *vosotros* and one with *usted, ustedes*.

1. Familiar Commands *(Tú; Vosotros)*
   Familiar commands are used with people to whom you would say *tú*. The singular is the same as the third person singular of the present indicative:

¡Habla (tú)!	Speak!
¡Come (tú)!	Eat!
¡Sube (tú)!	Go up!

The plural *vosotros, -as* is always formed by removing the *-r* of the infinitive and adding *-d*. Remember that this latter form is used only in Spain. (For plural commands, both formal and informal, see 2., below.)

I

hablar   to speak

SINGULAR:	*¡Habla (tú)!*	Speak!
PLURAL:	*¡Hablad (vosotros, -as)!*	Speak!

II

aprender   to learn

SINGULAR:	*¡Aprende (tú)!*	Learn!
PLURAL:	*¡Aprended (vosotros, -as)!*	Learn!

III

escribir   to write

SINGULAR:	*¡Escribe (tú)!*	Write!
PLURAL:	*¡Escribid (vosotros, -as)!*	Write!

Common exceptions in the singular (the plural is always regular):

		IMPERATIVE	
INFINITIVE		SINGULAR	PLURAL
ser	to be	*sé*	*sed*
decir	to say	*di*	*decid*
ir	to go	*ve*	*id*
hacer	to do	*haz*	*haced*
poner	to put	*pon*	*poned*
tener	to hold	*ten*	*tened*
venir	to come	*ven*	*venid*

Familiar commands in the negative are in the present subjunctive:

SINGULAR

¡No hables!	Don't speak!
¡No me hables!	Don't talk to me!
¡No comas!	Don't eat!

PLURAL

¡No habléis!	Don't speak!
¡No comáis!	Don't eat!

Other Examples:

¡Háblame!	Speak to me!
¡Háblales!	Speak to them!
¡No les hables!	Don't speak to them!
¡Hablad!	Speak!
¡No habléis!	Don't speak!
¡Dame!	Give me!
¡No me des!	Don't give me!
¡Dímelo!	Tell it to me!
¡No me lo digas (tú)!	Don't tell it to me!
¡No me digas (tú) eso!	Don't tell me that!
¡Decídnoslo!	Tell it to us!
¡No nos lo digáis!	Don't tell it to us!
¡No estudiéis demasiado!	Don't study too much!

Notice that the object pronouns follow the affirmative imperative and precede the negative imperative.

2. Polite Commands *(Usted)*

Polite commands are used with people to whom you would say *usted* and are formed like the subjunctive. You change the ending of the third person present indicative to *a* if it is *e*, or to *e* if it is *a*.

INDICATIVE		SUBJUNCTIVE	
Habla.	He speaks.	*Hable Ud.*	Speak!
Come.	He eats.	*Coma Ud.*	Eat!

The plural is formed by adding *n* to the singular of the imperative:

¡Hablen Uds.!	Speak!
¡Coman Uds.!	Eat!
¡Desciendan Uds.!	Go down!

Note that this form is used in Latin America to give commands to more than one person.

Other Examples:

¡Cómalo (Ud.)!	Eat it!
Venga (Ud.) a verme	Come to see me
¡Tómelo!	Take it!
¡Dígamelo!	Tell it to me!
Escríbame (Ud.) una carta	Write me a letter
¡Escríbamelo!	Write it to me!
¡Abra (Ud.) la ventana!	Open the window!

NEGATIVE

¡No hable Ud.!	Don't speak!
¡No lo coma Ud.!	Don't eat it!
¡No me lo diga Ud.!	Don't tell it to me!
¡No me escriba Ud.!	Don't write to me!
¡No hablen Uds. demasiado!	Don't talk too much!

The pronoun objects follow the affirmative imperative and are attached to it:

¡Léelo (tú)!	Read it!
¡Habladle!	Speak to him!
¡Véndamelo!	Sell it to me!
¡Dígamelo!	Tell it to me!

3. Indirect Commands
   Indirect commands are in the subjunctive and are usually preceded by *que:*

¡Que entren!	Let them come in!
¡Que él lo haga!	Let him do it!
¡Que lo haga Juan!	Let John do it!
¡Que le hable María!	Let Mary talk to him!
¡Que venga!	Let him come!
¡Que vaya él!	Let him go!
¡Que no venga!	Let him not come!
¡Viva España!	Long live Spain!
¡Dios guarde a nuestro país!	God keep our country!

4. "Let's" is expressed by the subjunctive:

¡Hablemos un rato!	Let's talk a while!
¡No hablemos!	Let's not talk!
¡Esperemos!	Let's wait!

Note:
¡Vamos!	Let's go!
¡No vayamos!	Let's not go!

5. Imperative of Reflexive Verbs
   The final *-d* of the plural is dropped when *-os* is added; that is, "*sentados*" becomes *sentaos:*

FAMILIAR FORM

SINGULAR

¡Siéntate!	Sit down!
¡Despiértate!	Wake up!
¡No te sientes!	Don't sit down!

PLURAL

¡Sentaos!	Sit down!
¡Despertaos!	Wake up!
(despertud + os)	
¡No os sentéis!	Don't sit down!

POLITE FORM

SINGULAR

¡Siéntese Ud.!	Sit down!
¡No se siente Ud.!	Don't sit down!

PLURAL

¡Siéntense Uds.!	Sit down *(pl.)*!
¡No se sienten!	Don't sit down!
¡Sentémonos!	Let's sit down!
(sentemos + nos)	

32. THE PARTICIPLE

1. The present participle (also called the "gerund")
   of Conjugation I is formed by dropping the *-ar*
   of the infinitive and adding *-ando;* the present
   participle of Conjugations II and III is made by
   dropping the *-er (-ir)* and adding *-iendo:*

I		II	
hablar	to speak	*comer*	to eat
hablando	speaking	*comiendo*	eating

III	
vivir	to live
viviendo	living

Pronoun objects are attached to the present participle (in such cases the verb has a written accent):

comprándolos	buying them
vendiéndomelo	selling it to me
dándoselo	giving it to him

The present participle is often used absolutely, describing some action or state of being of the subject of the sentence:

Durmiendo, no me oyeron.	Since they were sleeping, they didn't hear me. They didn't hear me because they were sleeping.
Estando cansados, dormían.	Being tired, they were sleeping. They were taking a nap because they were tired.

2. The past participle is formed by adding *-ado* to the stem of *-ar* verbs (that is, the infinitive minus *-ar*) and *-ido* to the stem of *-er* and *-ir* verbs:

I		II	
hablar	to speak	*comer*	to eat
hablado	spoken	*comido*	eaten

III	
vivir	to live
vivido	lived

3. Irregular Participles

The following are some of the most common verbs with irregular present and past participles:

INFINITIVE		IRREGULAR PAST PARTICIPLE	IRREGULAR PRESENT PARTICIPLE
abrir	to open	*abierto*	
caer	to fall	*caído*	*cayendo*
creer	to believe	*creído*	*creyendo*
cubrir	to cover	*cubierto*	
decir	to say	*dicho*	*diciendo*
despedirse	to take leave of		*despidiéndose*
dormir	to sleep	*dormido*	*dormiendo*
escribir	to write	*escrito*	
hacer	to do, make	*hecho*	
ir	to go		*yendo*
leer	to read	*leído*	*leyendo*
morir	to die	*muerto*	*muriendo*
oír	to hear		*oyendo*
pedir	to ask for		*pidiendo*
poder	to be able to		*pudiendo*
poner	to put	*puesto*	
seguir	to follow		*siguiendo*
sentir	to feel		*sintiendo*
traer	to bring	*traído*	*trayendo*
venir	to come		*viniendo*
ver	to see	*visto*	
volver	to return	*vuelto*	

33. Progressive Tenses

The Spanish progressive tenses are made up of the forms of *estar* plus the present participle. As in English, they denote a continuing action (that is, they describe the action as going on):

Estoy trabajando aquí.	I'm working here.
Estábamos leyendo un periódico.	We were reading a newspaper.

Estoy divertiéndome.	I'm having a good time.
Está hablando.	He's speaking
Estaba esperándome.	He was waiting for me.

34. Passive Voice

The passive voice is made up of the forms of *ser* plus the past participle:

| *La carta fue escrita por ella.* | The letter was written by her. |

The passive is used as in English. Very often, however, Spanish uses the reflexive where English uses the passive (see p. 84):

| *Aquí se habla inglés.* | English is spoken here. |

35. To Be

There are two verbs in Spanish for "to be": *ser* and *estar.* Here are the present tense forms of *ser* and *estar.* See "The Forms of Irregular Verbs" (p. 332–341) for other tenses.

SER	ESTAR	
yo soy	*yo estoy*	I am
tú eres	*tú estás*	you are
usted es	*usted está*	you are
él es	*él está*	he is
ella es	*ella está*	she is
nosotros somos	*nosotros estamos*	we are
nosotras somos	*nosotras estamos*	we are
vosotros sois	*vosotros estáis*	you are
vosotras sois	*vosotras estáis*	you are

ustedes son	ustedes están	you are
ellos son	ellos están	they are
ellas son	ellas están	they are

USAGES:

1. *Ser*

a. indicates a characteristic:

| *Mi hermano es alto.* | My brother is tall. |

b. is used with a predicate noun, in which case it links two equal things:

El es médico.	He is a doctor
Es escritor.	He's a writer.
Es español.	He's a Spaniard.

c. is used with an adjective to indicate an inherent quality.

El libro es rojo.	The book is red.
Ella es joven.	She is young
El hielo es frío.	Ice is cold.
Es inteligente.	He's intelligent.
Es encantadora.	She's charming.

d. is used with pronouns:

| *Soy yo.* | It's I. |

e. indicates origin, source, or material:

¿De dónde es Ud.?	Where are you from?
Soy de España.	I'm from Spain.
Es de madera.	It's made of wood.
Es de plata.	It's silver.

f. indicates possession:

¿De quién es esto?	Whose is this?
Los libros son del señor Díaz.	The books belong to Mr. Diaz.

g. is used in telling time:

Es la una.	It's one o'clock.
Son las dos.	It's two o'clock.
Son las nueve y diez.	It's ten past nine.

h. is used to indicate cost:

Son a ciento cincuenta pesetas la docena.	They are 150 pesetas a dozen.
Son a nueve balboas cada uno.	They are nine balboas each.

i. is used in impersonal constructions:

Es tarde.	It's late.
Es temprano.	It's early.
Es necesario.	It's necessary.
Es lástima.	It's a pity.
¿No es verdad?	Isn't it?

2. *Estar*

a. expresses position or location:

Está allí.	He's over there.
Está en México.	He's in Mexico.
Nueva York está en los Estados Unidos.	New York is in the United States.
Los Andes están en Sudamérica.	The Andes are in South America.
El Canal está en Panamá.	The Canal is in Panama.

| ¿Dónde está el libro? | Where's the book? |
| Está sobre la mesa. | It's on the table. |

    b. indicates a state or condition which may change:

Ella está contenta.	She's pleased.
Estoy cansado.	I'm tired.
Estoy listo.	I'm ready.
El café está frío.	The coffee's cold.
Está claro.	It's clear.
La ventana está abierta (cerrada).	The window's open (shut).

    c. is used to form the present progressive tense:

| Están hablando. | They are talking. |
| Están caminando. | They are walking. |

    d. is used to ask about or describe states or conditions of physical or mental health:

¿Cómo está Ud.?	How are you?
¿Cómo están ellos?	How are they?
Estamos tristes.	We're sad.
Están muertos.	They are dead.
Estoy enojada.	I'm angry.

    Some adjectives may be used with either *ser* or *estar* with a difference in meaning.

El es malo.	He is bad (an evil person).
El está malo.	He is sick.
Es pálida.	She has a pale complexion.
Está pálida.	She is pale (owing to illness).

	With *ser*	With *estar*
bueno	good	well, in good health
listo	clever	ready, prepared
cansado	tiresome	tired

THE FORMS OF THE REGULAR VERBS

CONJUGATIONS I, II, III

INDICATIVE

Infinitive	Pres. & Past Participles	Present Indicative	Imperfect	Preterite	Future	Conditional	Present Perfect	Pluperfect	Preterite Perfect
I. -ar ending *hablar* to speak	hablando hablado	hablo hablas habla hablamos habláis hablan	hablaba hablabas hablaba hablábamos hablabais hablaban	hablé hablaste habló hablamos hablasteis hablaron	hablaré hablarás hablará hablaremos hablaréis hablarán	hablaría hablarías hablaría hablaríamos hablaríais hablarían	he has ha + hablado hemos habéis han	había habías había + hablado habíamos habíais habían	hube hubiste hubo + hablado hubimos hubisteis hubieron
II. -er ending *comer* to eat	comiendo comido	como comes come comemos coméis comen	comía comías comía comíamos comíais comían	comí comiste comió comimos comisteis comieron	comeré comerás comerá comeremos comeréis comerán	comería comerías comería comeríamos comeríais comerían	he has ha + comido hemos habéis han	había habías había + comido habíamos habíais habían	hube hubiste hubo + comido hubimos hubisteis hubieron

INDICATIVE

Infinitive	Pres. & Past Participles	Present Indicative	Imperfect	Preterite	Future	Conditional	Present Perfect	Pluperfect	Preterite Perfect
III. -ir ending *vivir* to live	viviendo vivido	vivo vives vive vivimos vivís viven	vivía vivías vivía vivíamos vivíais vivían	viví viviste vivió vivimos vivisteis vivieron	viviré vivirás vivirá viviremos viviréis vivirán	viviría vivirías viviría viviríamos viviríais vivirían	he has ha + hemos habéis han ... vivido	había habías había + habíamos habíais habían ... vivido	hube hubiste hubo + hubimos hubisteis hubieron ... vivido

Future Perfect	Conditional Perfect	Present
habré habrás habrá + hablado habremos habréis habrán	habría habrías habría + hablado habríamos habríais habrían	hable hables hable hablemos habléis hablen

SUBJUNCTIVE

Imperfect (-r-)	Imperfect (-s-)	Present Perfect	Pluperfect (-r-)	Pluperfect (-s-)	Imperative
hablara hablaras hablara habláramos hablarais hablaran	hablase hablases hablase hablásemos hablaseis hablasen	haya hayas haya + hablado hayamos hayáis hayan	hubiera hubieras hubiera + hablado hubiéramos hubierais hubieran	hubiese hubieses hubiese + hablado hubiésemos hubieseis hubiesen	¡Habla (tú)! ¡Hable (Ud.)! ¡Hablemos (nosotros)! ¡Hablad (vosotros)! ¡Hablen (Uds.)!

306

INDICATIVE

SUBJUNCTIVE

Future Perfect	Conditional Perfect	Present	Imperfect (-r-)	Imperfect (-s-)	Present Perfect	Pluperfect (-r-)	Pluperfect (-s-)	Imperative
habré	habría	coma	comiera	comiese	haya	hubiera	hubiese	¡Come (tú)!
habrás	habrías	comas	comieras	comieses	hayas	hubieras	hubieses	¡Coma (Ud.)!
habrá + comido	habría + comido	coma	comiera	comiese	haya + comido	hubiera + comido	hubiese + comido	¡Comamos (nosotros)!
habremos	habríamos	comamos	comiéramos	comiésemos	hayamos	hubiéramos	hubiésemos	¡Comed (vosotros)!
habréis	habríais	comáis	comierais	comieseis	hayáis	hubierais	hubieseis	¡Coman (Uds.)!
habrán	habrían	coman	comieran	comiesen	hayan	hubieran	hubiesen	
habré	habría	viva	viviera	viviese	haya	hubiera	hubiese	¡Vive (tú)!
habrás	habrías	vivas	vivieras	vivieses	hayas	hubieras	hubieses	¡Viva (Ud.)!
habrá + vivido	habría + vivido	viva	viviera	viviese	haya + vivido	hubiera + vivido	hubiese + vivido	¡Vivamos (nosotros)!
habremos	habríamos	vivamos	viviéramos	viviésemos	hayamos	hubiéramos	hubiésemos	¡Vivid (vosotros)!
habréis	habríais	viváis	vivierais	vivieseis	hayáis	hubierais	hubieseis	¡Vivan (Uds.)!
habrán	habrían	vivan	vivieran	viviesen	hayan	hubieran	hubiesen	

Radical Changing Verbs

1. GROUP I: -AR AND -ER VERBS ONLY

a) Change the *o* to *ue* when stress falls on root (ex: *contar, volver*).
b) Change the *e* to *ie* when stress falls on root (ex: *pensar, perder*).

Infinitive*	Present Indicative	Present Subjunctive	Imperative	Similarly Conjugated Verbs		
contar(o>ue) to count	cuento cuentas cuenta contamos contáis cuentan	cuente cuentes cuente contemos contéis cuenten	cuenta contad	acordar acordarse acostarse almorzar apostar aprobar	avergonzar avergonzarse colgar costar encontrar jugar (*u to ue*)	probar recordar recordarse sonar volar volver
volver(o>ue) to return	vuelvo vuelves vuelve volvemos volvéis vuelven	vuelva vuelvas vuelva volvamos volváis vuelvan	vuelve volved	devolver doler dolerse llover morder mover	oler soler	

Infinitive*	Present Indicative	Present Subjunctive	Imperative	Similarly Conjugated Verbs		
pensar(e>ie) to think	pienso piensas piensa pensamos penséis piensan	piense pienses piense pensemos penséis piensen	piensa pensad	acertar apretar calentar cerrar confesar despertar	empezar encerrar gobernar plegar quebrar sentarse	temblar tentar
perder(e>ie) to lose	pierdo pierdes pierde perdemos perdéis pierden	pierda pierdas pierda perdamos perdáis pierdan	pierde perded	ascender atender defender descender encender entender	extender tender	

*In all the other tenses, these verbs are conjugated like all other regular verbs.

RADICAL CHANGING VERBS

2. GROUP II: -IR VERBS ONLY

a) Change *o* to *ue* when stress falls on root (ex: *dormir*).
b) Change *o* to *u*; a) when stress falls on ending (ex: *dormir*—present subj. only); b) in third persons of preterite.
c) Change *e* to *ie* when stress falls on root (ex: *sentir*).
d) Change *e* to *i*; a) when stress falls on ending (ex: *sentir*—present subj. only); b) in third persons of preterite.

Infinitive*	Present Indicative	Present Subjunctive	Preterite	Imperative	Similarly Conjugated Verbs	
dormir to sleep	duermo duermes duerme dormimos dormís duermen	duerma duermas duerma durmamos durmáis duerman	dormí dormiste durmió dormimos dormisteis durmieron	duerme dormid	morir (past participle: *muerto*)	
sentir to feel	siento sientes siente sentimos sentís sienten	sienta sientas sienta sintamos sintáis sientan	sentí sentiste sintió sentimos sentisteis sintieron	siente sentid	advertir arrepentirse consentir convertir diferir divertir	herir mentir preferir presentir referir sugerir

*In all the other tenses, these verbs are conjugated like all other regular verbs.

310

3. GROUP III: -IR VERBS ONLY

Change *e* to *i*; a) when stress falls on root; b) in third persons of preterite (ex: *pedir*)

Infinitive[†]	Present Indicative	Present Subjunctive	Preterite Indicative	Imperfect Subjunctive	Imperative	Similarly Conjugated Verbs	
pedir to ask	pido	pida	pedí	pidiera (se)	pide	competir	expedir
	pides	pidas	pediste	pidieras (ses)	pedid	conseguir	reír
	pide	pida	pidió	pidiera (se)		corregir	repetir
	pedimos	pidamos	pedimos	pidiéramos (semos)		despedir	seguir
	pedís	pidáis	pedisteis	pidiérais (seis)		despedirse	servir
	piden	pidan	pidieron	pidieran (sen)		elegir	vestir

[†]In all the other tenses, these verbs are conjugated like all other regular verbs.

REGULAR VERBS WITH SPELLING CHANGES

1. VERBS ENDING IN -CAR

Example: buscar to look for

Verbs ending in -*car; c* changes to *qu* when followed by *e*. This occurs in:

1. the first person singular of the preterite
2. all persons of the present subjunctive

PRETERITE INDICATIVE	PRESENT SUBJUNCTIVE
busqué	*busque*
buscaste	*busques*
buscó	*busque*
buscamos	*busquemos*
buscasteis	*busquéis*
buscaron	*busquen*

Verbs conjugated like *buscar:*

acercar	to place near	*sacrificar*	to sacrifice
educar	to educate	*secar*	to dry
explicar	to explain	*significar*	to signify, mean
fabricar	to manufacture	*tocar*	to touch, play (music)
indicar	to indicate		
pecar	to sin	*verificar*	to verify
sacar	to take out		

2. VERBS ENDING IN *-GAR*

Example: *pagar* to pay

Verbs ending in *-gar: g* changes to *gu* when followed by *e*. This occurs in:

1. the first person singular of the preterite indicative
2. all persons of the present subjunctive

PRETERITE INDICATIVE	PRESENT SUBJUNCTIVE
pagué	*pague*
pagaste	*pagues*
pagó	*pague*
pagamos	*paguemos*
pagasteis	*paguéis*
pagaron	*paguen*

Verbs conjugated like *pagar:*

ahogar	to drown	*investigar*	to investigate
apagar	to extinguish	*juzgar*	to judge
arriesgar	to risk	*llegar*	to arrive
cargar	to load	*obligar*	to compel
castigar	to punish	*otorgar*	to grant
congregar	to congregate	*pegar*	to hit
entregar	to deliver	*tragar*	to swallow

3. VERBS ENDING IN -*GUAR*

Example: averiguar to ascertain, investigate

Verbs ending in -*guar: gu* changes to *gü* when followed by *e*. This occurs in:

1. the first person singular of the preterite indicative
2. all persons of the present subjunctive

PRETERITE INDICATIVE	PRESENT SUBJUNCTIVE
averigüé	*averigüe*
averiguaste	*averigües*
averiguó	*averigüe*
averiguamos	*averigüemos*
averiguasteis	*averigüéis*
averiguaron	*averigüen*

Verbs conjugated like *averiguar:*

aguar	to water, dilute
atestiguar	to attest

4. VERBS ENDING IN -*ZAR*

Example: *gozar* to enjoy

Verbs ending in -*zar: z* changes to *c* when followed by *e*. This occurs in:

1. the first person singular of the preterite indicative
2. all persons of the present subjunctive

PRETERITE INDICATIVE	PRESENT SUBJUNCTIVE
gocé	*goce*
gozaste	*goces*
gozó	*goce*
gozamos	*gocemos*
gozasteis	*goséis*
gozaron	*gocen*

Verbs conjugated like *gozar:*

abrazar	to embrace	*organizar*	to organize
alcanzar	to reach	*rechazar*	to reject
cruzar	to cross	*rezar*	to pray
enlazar	to join	*utilizar*	to utilize

5. VERBS ENDING IN -*GER*

Example: *coger* to catch

Verbs ending in -*ger*: *g* changes to *j* when followed by *o* or *a*. This occurs in:

1. the first person singular of the present indicative
2. all persons of the present subjunctive

PRESENT INDICATIVE	PRESENT SUBJUNCTIVE
cojo	*coja*
coges	*cojas*
coge	*coja*
cogemos	*cojamos*
cogéis	*cojáis*
cogen	*cojan*

Verbs conjugated like *coger:*

acoger	to welcome	*proteger*	to protect
escoger	to choose, select	*recoger*	to gather

6. VERBS ENDING IN *-GIR*

Example: *dirigir* to direct

Verbs ending in *-gir:* *g* changes to *j* when followed by *o* or *a*. This occurs in:

1. the first person singular of the present indicative
2. all persons of the present subjunctive

PRESENT INDICATIVE

PRESENT SUBJUNCTIVE

dirijo	*dirija*
diriges	*dirijas*
dirige	*dirija*
dirigimos	*dirijamos*
dirigís	*dirijáis*
dirigen	*dirijan*

Verbs conjugated like *dirigir:*

afligir	to afflict	*rugir*	to roar
erigir	to erect	*surgir*	to come forth
exigir	to demand		

7. VERBS ENDING IN *-GUIR*

Example: *distinguir* to distinguish

Verbs ending in *-guir:* *gu* changes to *g* when followed by *o* or *a*. This occurs in:

1. the first person singular of the present indicative
2. all persons of the present subjunctive

PRESENT INDICATIVE	PRESENT SUBJUNCTIVE
distingo	*distinga*
distingues	*distingas*
distingue	*distinga*
distinguimos	*distingamos*
distinguís	*distingáis*
distinguen	*distingan*

Verbs conjugated like *distinguir:*

conseguir	to get, obtain	*perseguir*	to persecute
extinguir	to extinguish	*seguir*	to follow

8. VERBS ENDING IN -*CER, -CIR*

(Preceded by a vowel)

Examples: *conocer* to know   *lucir* to shine

Verbs ending in -*cre, -cir*, preceded by a vowel, change *c* to *zc* before *o* or *a*. This occurs in:

1. the first person singular of the present indicative
2. all persons of the present subjunctive

INDICATIVE	SUBJUNCTIVE	INDICATIVE	SUBJUNCTIVE
conozco	*conozca*	*luzco*	*luzca*
conoces	*conozcas*	*luces*	*luzcas*
conoce	*conozca*	*luce*	*luzca*
conocemos	*conozcamos*	*lucimos*	*luzcamos*
conocéis	*conozcáis*	*lucís*	*luzcáis*
conocen	*conozcan*	*lucen*	*luzcan*

Verbs conjugated like *conocer:*

aborrecer	to hate	*desaparecer*	to disappear
acaecer	to happen	*desobe-decer*	to disobey
acontecer	to happen	*desvanecer*	to vanish
agradecer	to be grate-ful	*embellecer*	to embel-lish
amanecer	to dawn	*envejecer*	to grow old
anochecer	to grow dark	*fallecer*	to die
aparecer	to appear	*favorecer*	to favor
carecer	to lack	*merecer*	to merit
compadecer	to pity	*nacer*	to be born
complacer	to please	*obedecer*	to obey
conducir	to conduct, to drive	*ofrecer*	to offer
crecer	to grow	*oscurecer*	to grow dark
padecer	to suffer	*placer*	to please
parecer	to seem	*reconocer*	to recog-nize
permanecer	to last	*traducir*	to translate
pertenecer	to belong to		

9. VERBS ENDING IN *-CER*

(Preceded by a Consonant)

Example: *vencer* to conquer

Verbs ending in *-cer,* preceded by a consonant: *c* changes to *z* when followed by *e* or *a*. This occurs in:

1. the first person singular of the present indicative
2. all persons of the present subjunctive

PRESENT INDICATIVE	PRESENT SUBJUNCTIVE
venzo	*venza*
vences	*venzas*
vence	*venza*
vencemos	*venzamos*
vencéis	*venzáis*
vencen	*venzan*

Verbs conjugated like *vencer:*

convencer   to convince   *ejercer*   to exercise

10. VERBS ENDING IN *-UIR*

(But not *-guir* and *-quir*)

Example: *construir* to build

Verbs ending in *-uir,* except those ending in *-guir* or *-quir,* add *y* to the stem of the verb before *a, e, o.* This occurs in:

1. all persons of the present indicative (except the first and second familiar persons plural)
2. all persons of the present and imperfect subjunctive
3. the imperative singular *(tú)*
4. third singular and plural of the preterite

PRESENT INDICATIVE	PRESENT SUBJUNCTIVE
construyo	*construya*
construyes	*construyas*
construye	*construya*
construimos	*construyamos*
construís	*construyáis*
construyen	*construyan*

(*i* between two other vowels changes to *y*)

PRETERITE INDICATIVE	IMPERFECT SUBJUNCTIVE
construí	*construyera (se)*
construiste	*construyeras (ses)*
construyó	*construyera (se)*
construimos	*construyéramos (semos)*
construisteis	*construyerais (seis)*
construyeron	*construyeran (sen)*

IMPERATIVE
construye
construid

Verbs conjugated like *construir:*

atribuir	to attribute	*huir*	to flee
constituir	to constitute	*influir*	to influence
contribuir	to contribute	*instruir*	to instruct
destituir	to deprive	*reconstruir*	to rebuild
destruir	to destroy	*restituir*	to restore
distribuir	to distribute	*substituir*	to substitute
excluir	to exclude		

11. VERBS LIKE *CREER*

Creer to believe

In verbs whose stem ends in *e,* the *i* of the regular endings beginning with *-ie, -ió,* becomes *y.* This occurs in:

1. the present participle *creyendo.*
2. the third person singular and plural of the preterite indicative

3. both forms of the imperfect subjunctive

PRETERITE INDICATIVE	IMPERFECT SUBJUNCTIVE
creí	*creyera (se)*
creiste	*creyeras (ses)*
creyó	*creyera (se)*
creimos	*creyéramos (semos)*
creísteis	*creyerais (seis)*
creyeron	*creyeran (sen)*

Verbs conjugated like *creer:*

caer	to fall (irregular)	*leer*	to read
construir	to build	*poseer*	to possess

12. VERBS LIKE *REÍR*

Reír to laugh

In verbs whose stem ends in *i*, the *i* of the regular endings, *-ie*, *-ió*, is dropped to avoid two *i*'s. This occurs in:

1. the present participle *riendo*
2. the third person singular and plural of the preterite indicative
3. all persons of both forms of the imperfect subjunctive

PRETERITE INDICATIVE	IMPERFECT SUBJUNCTIVE
reí	*riera (se)*
reiste	*rieras (ses)*
rió	*riera (se)*

reímos	*riéramos (semos)*
reísteis	*rierais (seis)*
rieron	*rieran (sen)*

Verbs conjugated like *reír; sonreír* to smile.

13. VERBS ENDING IN *-LLER, -LLIR, -ÑER, -ÑIR*

Example: *tañer* to toll (a bell)
PRESENT PARTICIPLE: *tañendo*

PRETERITE	IMPERFECT
INDICATIVE	SUBJUNCTIVE
tañí	*tañera (se)*
tañiste	*tañeras (ses)*
tañó	*tañera (se)*
tañimos	tañéramos (semos)
tañisteis	tañerais (seis)
tañeron	tañeran (sen)

In verbs whose stem ends in *ll* or *ñ*, the *i* of the regular endings beginning with *-ie, -ió* is dropped. This occurs in:

1. the present participle
2. the third person singular and plural of the preterite indicative
3. all persons of both forms of the imperfect subjunctive

Verbs conjugated like *tañer:*

bullir	to boil	*gruñir*	to growl

14. VERBS ENDING IN *-IAR, -UAR*

Examples: *enviar* to send   *continuar* to continue

PRES. IND.	PRES. SUBJ.	PRES. IND.	PRES. SUBJ.
envío	*envíe*	*continúo*	*continúe*
envías	*envíes*	*continúas*	*continúes*
envía	*envíe*	*continúa*	*continúe*
enviamos	*enviemos*	*continuamos*	*continuemos*
enviáis	*enviéis*	*continuáis*	*continuéis*
envían	*envíen*	*continúan*	*continúen*

	IMPERATIVE
envía	*continúa*
enviad	*continuad*

Some verbs ending in *-iar* or *-uar* take a written accent over the *i* or the *u* of the stem.

1. in all persons of the present indicative (except the first plural and second plural familiar).
2. in all persons of the present subjunctive (except the first plural and the second plural familiar).
3. in the singular of the imperative *(tú)*.

Verbs conjugated like *enviar:*

confiar	to trust	*desconfiar*	to distrust
criar	to bring up	*fiar*	to give credit
desafiar	to challenge	*guiar*	to guide

Verbs conjugated like *continuar:*

actuar	to act	*evaluar*	to evaluate
efectuar	to carry out	*perpetuar*	to perpetuate

THE FORMS OF THE IRREGULAR VERBS*

Infinitive Present and Past Participles	Present Indicative	Present Subjunctive	Imperfect	Preterite	Future	Conditional	Imperative
andar "to walk"	ando	ande	andaba	anduve	andaré	andaría	anda
andando	andas	andes	andabas	anduviste	andarás	andarías	andad
andado	anda	ande	andaba	anduvo	andará	andaría	
	andamos	andemos	andábamos	anduvimos	andaremos	andaríamos	
	andáis	andéis	andabais	anduvisteis	andaréis	andaríais	
	andan	anden	andaban	anduvieron	andarán	andarían	
caber "to fit," "to be contained in"	quepo	quepa	cabía	cupe	cabré	cabría	cabe
	cabes	quepas	cabías	cupiste	cabrás	cabrías	cabed
	cabe	quepa	cabía	cupo	cabrá	cabría	
	cabemos	quepamos	cabíamos	cupimos	cabremos	cabríamos	
cabiendo	cabéis	quepáis	cabíais	cupisteis	cabréis	cabríais	
cabido	caben	quepan	cabían	cupieron	cabrán	cabrían	

Infinitive	Present Indicative	Present Subjunctive	Imperfect	Preterite	Future	Conditional	Imperative
caer "to fall" *cayendo* *caído*	caigo caes cae caemos caéis caen	caiga caigas caiga caigamos caigáis caigan	caía caías caía caíamos caíais caían	caí caíste cayó caímos caísteis cayeron	caeré caerás caerá caeremos caeréis caerán	caería caerías caería caeríamos caeríais caerían	cae caed
conducir "to lead," "to drive" *conduciendo* *conducido*	conduzco conduces conduce conducimos conducís conducen	conduzca conduzcas conduzca conduzcamos conduzcáis conduzcan	conducía conducías conducía conducíamos conducíais conducían	conduje condujiste condujo condujimos condujisteis condujeron	conduciré conducirás conducirá conduciremos conduciréis conducirán	conduciría conducirías conduciría conduciríamos conduciríais conducirían	conduce conducid
dar "to give" *dando* *dado*	doy das da damos dais dan	dé des dé demos deis den	daba dabas daba dábamos dabais daban	di diste dio dimos disteis dieron	daré darás dará daremos daréis darán	daría darías daría daríamos daríais darían	da dad

THE FORMS OF THE IRREGULAR VERBS*

Infinitive Present and Past Participles	Present Indicative	Present Subjunctive	Imperfect	Preterite	Future	Conditional	Imperative
decir "to say," "to tell"	digo	diga	decía	dije	diré	diría	di
diciendo	dices	digas	decías	dijiste	dirás	dirías	decid
dicho	dice	diga	decía	dijo	dirá	diría	
	decimos	digamos	decíamos	dijimos	diremos	diríamos	
	decís	digáis	decíais	dijisteis	diréis	diríais	
	dicen	digan	decían	dijeron	dirán	dirían	
estar "to be"	estoy	esté	estaba	estuve	estaré	estaría	está
estando	estás	estés	estabas	estuviste	estarás	estarías	estad
estado	está	esté	estaba	estuvo	estará	estaría	
	estamos	estemos	estábamos	estuvimos	estaremos	estaríamos	
	estáis	estéis	estábais	estuvisteis	estaréis	estaríais	
	están	estén	estaban	estuvieron	estarán	estarían	

	Present	Subjunctive	Imperfect	Preterite	Future	Conditional	Command
haber "to have" (auxiliary)	he	haya	había	hube	habré	habría	
	has	hayas	habías	hubiste	habrás	habrías	
	ha	haya	había	hubo	habrá	habría	
	hemos	hayamos	habíamos	hubimos	habremos	habríamos	
	habéis	hayáis	habíais	hubisteis	habréis	habríais	
	han	hayan	habían	hubieron	habrán	habrían	
habiendo							
habido							
hacer "to do," "to make"	hago	haga	hacía	hice	haré	haría	haz
	haces	hagas	hacías	hiciste	harás	harías	haced
	hace	haga	hacía	hizo	hará	haría	
	hacemos	hagamos	hacíamos	hicimos	haremos	haríamos	
	hacéis	hagáis	hacíais	hicisteis	haréis	haríais	
	hacen	hagan	hacían	hicieron	harán	harían	
haciendo							
hecho							
ir "to go"	voy	vaya	iba	fui	iré	iría	ve
	vas	vayas	ibas	fuiste	irás	irías	id
	va	vaya	iba	fue	irá	iría	
	vamos	vayamos	íbamos	fuimos	iremos	iríamos	
	vais	vayáis	ibais	fuisteis	iréis	iríais	
	van	vayan	iban	fueron	irán	irían	
yendo							
ido							

THE FORMS OF THE IRREGULAR VERBS*

Infinitive Present and Past Participles	Present Indicative	Present Subjunctive	Imperfect	Preterite	Future	Conditional	Imperative
oír "to hear"	oigo	oiga	oía	oí	oiré	oiría	oye
oyendo	oyes	oigas	oías	oíste	oirás	oirías	oíd
oído	oye	oiga	oía	oyó	oirá	oiría	
	oímos	oigamos	oíamos	oímos	oiremos	oiríamos	
	oís	oigáis	oíais	oísteis	oiréis	oiríais	
	oyen	oigan	oían	oyeron	oirán	oirían	
poder "to be able," "can"	puedo	pueda	podía	pude	podré	podría	puede
pudiendo	puedes	puedas	podías	pudiste	podrás	podrías	poded
podido	puede	pueda	podía	pudo	podrá	podría	
	podemos	podamos	podíamos	pudimos	podremos	podríamos	
	podéis	podáis	podíais	pudisteis	podréis	podríais	
	pueden	puedan	podían	pudieron	podrán	podrían	

328

	Present	Pres. Subj.	Imperfect	Preterite	Future	Conditional	Imperative
poner "to put," "to place" *poniendo* *puesto*	pongo	ponga	ponía	puse	pondré	pondría	
	pones	pongas	ponías	pusiste	pondrás	pondrías	pon
	pone	ponga	ponía	puso	pondrá	pondría	poned
	ponemos	pongamos	poníamos	pusimos	pondremos	pondríamos	
	ponéis	pongáis	poníais	pusisteis	pondréis	pondríais	
	ponen	pongan	ponían	pusieron	pondrán	pondrían	
querer "to want," "to love" *queriendo* *querido*	quiero	quiera	quería	quise	querré	querría	
	quieres	quieras	querías	quisiste	querrás	querrías	quiere
	quiere	quiera	quería	quiso	querrá	querría	quered
	queremos	queramos	queríamos	quisimos	querremos	querríamos	
	queréis	queráis	queríais	quisisteis	querréis	querríais	
	quieren	quieran	querían	quisieron	querrán	querrían	
reir "to laugh" *riendo* *reido*	río	ría	reía	reí	reiré	reiría	
	ríes	rías	reías	reíste	reirás	reirías	ríe
	ríe	ría	reía	rió	reirá	reiría	reíd
	reímos	ríamos	reíamos	reímos	reiremos	reiríamos	
	reís	riáis	reíais	reísteis	reiréis	reiríais	
	ríen	rían	reían	rieron	reirán	reirían	

THE FORMS OF THE IRREGULAR VERBS*

Infinitive Present and Past Participles	Present Indicative	Present Subjunctive	Imperfect	Preterite	Future	Conditional	Imperative
saber "to know" *sabiendo* *sabido*	sé	sepa	sabía	supe	sabré	sabría	sabe
	sabes	sepas	sabías	supiste	sabrás	sabrías	sabed
	sabe	sepa	sabía	supo	sabrá	sabría	
	sabemos	sepamos	sabíamos	supimos	sabremos	sabríamos	
	sabéis	sepáis	sabíais	supisteis	sabréis	sabríais	
	saben	sepan	sabían	supieron	sabrán	sabrían	
salir "to go out," "to leave" *saliendo* *salido*	salgo	salga	salía	salí	saldré	saldría	sal
	sales	salgas	salías	saliste	saldrás	saldrías	salid
	sale	salga	salía	salió	saldrá	saldría	
	salimos	salgamos	salíamos	salimos	saldremos	saldríamos	
	salís	salgáis	salíais	salisteis	saldréis	saldríais	
	salen	salgan	salían	salieron	saldrán	saldrían	

Infinitive / Participles	Present	Subjunctive	Imperfect	Preterite	Future	Conditional	Imperative
ser "to be" *siendo* *sido*	soy eres es somos sois son	sea seas sea seamos seáis sean	era eras era éramos erais eran	same as preterite of *ir.*	seré serás será seremos seréis serán	sería serías sería seríamos seríais serían	sé sed
tener "to have" *teniendo* *tenido*	tengo tienes tiene tenemos tenéis tienen	tenga tengas tenga tengamos tengáis tengan	tenía tenías tenía teníamos teníais tenían	tuve tuviste tuvo tuvimos tuvisteis tuvieron	tendré tendrás tendrá tendremos tendréis tendrán	tendría tendrías tendría tendríamos tendríais tendrían	ten tened
traer "to bring" *trayendo* *traído*	traigo traes trae traemos traéis traen	traiga traigas traiga traigamos traigáis traigan	traía traías traía traíamos traíais traían	traje trajiste trajo trajimos trajisteis trajeron	traeré traerás traerá traeremos traeréis traerán	traería traerías traería traeríamos traeríais traerían	trae traed

331

THE FORMS OF THE IRREGULAR VERBS*

Infinitive Present and Past Participles	Present Indicative	Present Subjunctive	Imperfect	Preterite	Future	Conditional	Imperative
valer "to be worth"	valgo	valga	valía	valí	valdré	valdría	val
valiendo	vales	valgas	valías	valiste	valdrás	valdrías	valed
valido	vale	valga	valía	valió	valdrá	valdría	
	valemos	valgamos	valíamos	valimos	valdremos	valdríamos	
	valéis	valgáis	valíais	valisteis	valdréis	valdríais	
	valen	valgan	valían	valieron	valdrán	valdrían	

	Present	Pres. Subj.	Imperfect	Preterite	Future	Conditional	Imperative
venir "to come"	vengo	venga	venía	vine	vendré	vendría	
viniendo	vienes	vengas	venías	viniste	vendrás	vendrías	ven
venido	viene	venga	venía	vino	vendrá	vendría	
	venimos	vengamos	veníamos	vinimos	vendremos	vendríamos	
	venís	vengáis	veníais	vinisteis	vendréis	vendríais	venid
	vienen	vengan	venían	vinieron	vendrán	vendrían	
ver "to see"	veo	vea	veía	vi	veré	vería	
viendo	ves	veas	veías	viste	verás	verías	ve
visto	ve	vea	veía	vio	verá	vería	
	vemos	veamos	veíamos	vimos	veremos	veríamos	
	veis	veáis	veíais	visteis	veréis	veríais	ved
	ven	vean	veían	vieron	verán	verían	

*To form compound tenses, use the appropriate form of *haber* together with the past participle of the irregular verb.

333

LETTER WRITING

Formal Invitations and Responses

INVITATIONS

marzo de 1993

Jorge Fernández y Sra.—Tienen el gusto de participar a Ud. y familia el próximo enlace matrimonial de su hija Carmen, con el Sr. Juan García y los invitan a la Ceremonia que se verificará en la Iglesia de Nuestra Señora de la Merced, el día 6 de este mes, a las 6 de la tarde. A continuación tendrá lugar una recepción en la casa de los padres de la novia en honor de los contrayentes.

March 1993

Mr. and Mrs. George Fernandez take pleasure in announcing the wedding of their daughter Carmen to Mr. Juan Garcia, and invite you to the ceremony that will take place at the Church of Nuestra Señora de la Merced, on the 6th of this month and year at 6 p.m. There will be a reception for the newlyweds afterward at the residence of the bride's parents.

Los señores Suárez ofrecen sus respetos a los señores García y les ruegan que les honren viniendo a comer con ellos el lunes próximo, a las ocho.

Mr. and Mrs. Suárez present their respects to Mr. and Mrs. García and would be honored to have their company at dinner next Monday at 8 o'clock.

Los señores Suárez y Navarro saludan afectuosamente a los señores Del Vayo y les ruegan que les hon-

*ren asistiendo a la recepción que darán en honor de
su hija María, el domingo 19 de marzo, a las nueve de
la noche.*

Mr. and Mrs. Suarez y Navarro ("greet Mr. and Mrs.
Del Vayo cordially and") request the honor of their
presence at the party given in honor of their daughter
Maria, on Sunday evening, March 19, at nine o'clock.

RESPONSES

*Los señores Del Vayo les agradecen infinito la
invitación que se han dignado hacerles y tendrán el
honor de asistir a la recepción del domingo 19 de
marzo.*

Thank you for your kind invitation. We shall be
honored to attend the reception on Sunday, March
19th.

*Los señores García tendrán el honor de acudir a la
cena de los señores Suárez y entretanto les saludan
cordialmente.*

Mr. and Mrs. García will be honored to have dinner
with Mr. and Mrs. Suárez. With kindest regards.

*Los señores García ruegan a los señores Suárez se
sirvan recibir las gracias por su amable invitación y
la expresión de su sentimiento al no poder aceptarla
por hallarse comprometidos con anterioridad.*

Mr. and Mrs. García thank Mr. and Mrs. Suárez for their kind invitation and regret that they are unable to come owing to a previous engagement.

Thank-You Notes

5 de marzo de 1993

Querida Anita,

La presente es con el fin de saludarte y darte las gracias por el precioso florero que me has enviado de regalo. Lo he colocado encima del piano y no te imaginas el lindo efecto que hace.

Espero verte pasado mañana en la fiesta que da Carmen, la cual parece que va a ser muy animada.

Deseo que estés bien en compañía de los tuyos. Nosotros sin novedad. Te saluda cariñosamente, tu amiga.

Lolita

March 5, 1993

Dear Anita,

This is just to say hello and also to let you know that I received the beautiful vase you sent me as a gift. I've put it on the piano and you can't imagine the beautiful effect.

I hope to see you at Carmen's party tomorrow. I think it's going to be a very lively affair.

I hope your family is all well. Everyone here is fine.

Lolita

Business Letters

Aranjo y Cía.
Paseo de Gracia, 125
Barcelon—España

2 de abril de 1993

González e hijos
Madrid—España

Muy señores nuestros:
Nos es grato presentarles al portador de la pre-
sente, Sr. Carlos de la Fuente, nuestro viajante, quien
está por visitar a las principales ciudades de esa
región. No necesitamos decirles que cualquier aten-
ción que le dispensen la consideraremos como un
favor personal. Anticipándoles las gracias, nos es
grato reiterarnos de Uds. como siempre,

Sus Attos. y SS.SS.
Aranjo y Cía.

———

Presidente.

Aranjo & Co., Inc.
125 Paseo de Gracia
Barcelona—Spain
April 2, 1993

Gonzalez & Sons
Madrid
Spain

Gentlemen:
We have the pleasure of introducing to you the
bearer of this letter, Mr. Carlos de la Fuente, one of

our salesmen, who is visiting the principal cities of your region. Needless to say, we shall greatly appreciate any courtesy you extend to him. ("It is needless to say to you that we shall consider any courtesy you extend him as a personal favor.") Thanking you in advance, we remain

Very truly yours,
Aranjo & Co., Inc.

———————————

President

Panamá
3 de marzo de 1993

Sr. Julián Pérez
Buenos Aires, 90, Apto. 22
Córdoba, Argentina

Muy señor mío:

Sírvase encontrar adjunto un cheque de $15 por un año de subscripción a la revista de su digna dirección.

Atentamente,

María Pérez de Perera
Apartado 98
Panamá, Rep. de Panamá

P.O. Box 98
Panama, Republic of Panama
March 3rd, 1993

Mr. Julian Perez
Buenos Aires, 90
P.O. Box 22
Córdoba, Argentina

Dear Sir:
  Enclosed please find a check for $15.00 for a year's
subscription to your magazine.

Very truly yours,
Mrs. María Perera

INFORMAL LETTERS

Mi querido Pepe:
  *Me ha sido sumamente grato recibir tu última
carta. Ante todo déjame darte la gran noticia. Pues he
decidido por fin hacer un viaje a Madrid, donde
pienso pasar todo el mes de mayo.*
  *Lolita viene conmigo. A ella le encanta la idea de
conoceros por fin.*
  *Los negocios marchan bien por ahora y confío en
que continuará la buena racha. El otro día estuve con
Antonio y me preguntó por ti.*
  *Procura mandar a reservarnos una habitación en el
Nacional, que te lo agradeceré mucho.*
  *Escríbeme pronto. Da mis recuerdos a Elena y tú
recibe un abrazo de tu amigo,*

Juan

Dear Pepe,
  I was very happy to get your last letter. First of all,
let me give you the big news. I have finally decided to

make a trip to Madrid, where I expect to spend all of May.

Lolita is coming with me. She is extremely happy to be able to meet the two of you at last.

Business is good now and I hope will keep up that way ("that the good wind will continue"). I saw Antonio the other day and he asked me about you.

I'd appreciate your trying to reserve a room for us in the "National."

Write soon. Give my regards to Elena.

Yours,
Juan

FORMS OF SALUTATIONS AND COMPLIMENTARY CLOSINGS

A. Salutations:

FORMAL

Señor:	Sir:
Señora:	Madam:
Señorita:	Miss:
Muy señor mío:	Dear Sir:
Muy señores míos:	Gentlemen:
Estimado señor:	Dear Sir:
De mi consideración:	Dear Sir:
Muy distinguido señor:	Dear Sir:
Muy señor nuestro:	Dear Sir:
Muy señores nuestros:	Gentlemen:
Señor profesor:	My dear Professor:
Excelentísimo señor:	Dear Sir: ("Your Excellency:")
Estimado amigo:	Dear Friend:
Querido amigo:	Dear Friend:

INFORMAL

Don Antonio (Aguilera);	My dear Mr. Aguilera:
Doña María (de Suárez):	My dear Mrs. Suárez:
Señorita Lolita (Suárez).	My dear Miss Suárez:
Antonio:	Anthony:
Querida Lolita.	Dear Lolita.
Mi querida Lolita.	My dear Lolita.
Amada mía:	My beloved:
Querida mía:	My dear,; My beloved:

B. Complimentary Closings:

FORMAL

The following are equivalent to our "Very sincerely yours":

Su Atto. y S.S. (Su atento y seguro servidor)

Sus Attos. y Ss. Ss. (Sus atentos y seguros servidores)

S.S.S. (Su seguro servidor)

Ss. Ss. Ss. (Sus seguros servidores)

INFORMAL

Cariñosamente.	Affectionately yours,
Atentamente.	Sincerely yours,
Sinceramente.	Sincerely yours,
Afectuosamente.	Affectionately yours,
Quien mucho le aprecia.	Affectionately,
De quien te estima.	Affectionately,
De su amigo que le quiere.	Affectionately,
De tu querida hija.	Your loving daughter,

Besos y abrazos
De todo corazón. }   With love,
De quien la adora.

C. Form of the Letter:

FORMAL

Estimado Señor:
or *Muy señor mío:*
(Dear Sir:)

———————————————————————
———————————————————————
———————————————————————

Atto. y S.S.[1]
(Yours truly,)

INFORMAL

Querido Juan:
(Dear John,)

———————————————————————
———————————————————————
———————————————————————

Cariñosamente,
(Affectionately,)
or
Afectuosamente,
(Affectionately,)

---

[1] *Atto. y S.S.* stands for *atento y seguro servidor.*

D. Common formulas:

Beginning a letter—

1. *Me es grato acusar recibo de su atenta del 8 de este mes. Tengo el agrado de* . . . This is to acknowledge receipt of your letter of the 8th of this month. I am glad to . . .

2. *Obra en mi poder su apreciable carta de fecha 10 de marzo* . . . I have received your letter of March 10th.

3. *En contestación a su atenta carta de* . . . In answer to your letter of . . .

4. *De conformidad con su carta del* . . . In accordance with your letter of . . .

5. *Con referencia a su anuncio en "La Nación" de hoy* . . . In reference to your ad in today's issue of "The Nation," . . .

6. *Por la presente me dirijo a Ud. para* . . . This letter is to . . .

7. *Nos es grato anunciarle que* . . . We are pleased to announce that . . .

8. *Me es grato recomendarle a Ud. al Sr.* . . . I take pleasure in recommending to you Mr. . . .

9. *La presente tiene por objeto confirmarle nuestra conversación telefónica de esta mañana* . . . This is to confirm our telephone conversation of this morning . . .

Ending a letter—

1. *Anticipándole las gracias, le saludo a Ud. atentamente,*
   Thanking you in advance, I am.
   > Sincerely yours,

2. *Anticipándoles las más expresivas gracias, quedamos de Uds.*
   > *Attos. y SS.SS.*
   Thanking you in advance, We are.
   > Sincerely yours,

3. *Quedamos de Ud. atentos y Ss. Ss.*
   We remain
   > Sincerely yours,

4. *En espera de sus gratas noticias, me repito de Ud.*
   > *Atento y S.S.*
   Hoping to hear from you, I am
   > Sincerely yours,

5. *Esperando su grata y pronta contestación, quedo,*
   > *Su atento y S.S.*
   Hoping to hear from you at your earliest convenience, I am
   > Sincerely yours,

The following are often used when beginning a business correspondence:

6. *Aprovecho esta ocasión para ofrecerme su atento y S.S.*
   I am taking advantage of this opportunity to introduce myself.

7. *Aprovechamos esta ocasión para suscribirnos,*
                                    Sus atentos y SS.SS.
We are taking this opportunity to introduce our-
selves.

FORM OF THE ENVELOPE

Félix Valbueña y Cía
Calle de Zurbarán, 6
Madrid

        Señor Don
        Ricardo Fitó,
        Apartado 5042,
        Barcelona

M. Navarro Suárez
San Martín Vía Aérea 820
Buenos Aires, Argentina

    Señores
    M. Suárez y Coello,
    Paseo de la Castellana, 84
    28002 Madrid, España

Señorita
Lolita Navarro
Gran Vía de Germanías, 63
Valencia

Antonio de Suárez
Calle del Sol, 2
(Chamartín)
Madrid

OTHER EXAMPLES

Sr. Don Antonio Aguilar [1]
Provenza, 95
Barcelona

Señorita
María Sucre y Navarro
Paseo de la Castellana, 80
Madrid

[1] To a doctor: *Sr. Dr. Antonio Aguilar.*
   To an engineer: *Sr. Ing. Don Antonio Aguilar.*